Praise for Mike Sager

"Sager plays Virgil in the modern American Inferno . . . Compelling and stylish magazine journalism, rich in novelistic detail."

—Kirkus Reviews

"Like his journalistic precursors Tom Wolfe and Hunter S. Thompson, Sager writes frenetic, off-kilter pop-sociological profiles of Americans in all their vulgarity and vitality . . . He writes with flair, but only in the service of an omnivorous curiosity and defies expectations in pieces that lesser writers would play for satire or sensationalism . . . A Whitmanesque ode to teeming humanity's mystical unity."

—The New York Times Book Review

"Sager's writing is strikingly perceptive. He writes like a novelist, stocking his stories with the details and observations other journalists might toss away."

—KPBS Radio's Culture Lust blog

"Mike Sager writes about places and events we seldom get a look at—and people from whom we avert our eyes. But with Sager in command of all the telling details, he shows us history, humanity, humor, sometimes even honor. He makes us glad to live with our eyes wide open."

—Richard Ben Cramer, Pulitzer Prize-winning author of
What It Takes: The Way to the White House

"Mike Sager is the Beat poet of American journalism, that rare reporter who can make literature out of shabby reality. Equal parts reporter, ethnographer, stylist and cultural critic, Sager has for 20 years carried the tradition of Tom Wolfe on his broad shoulders, chronicling the American scene and psyche. Nobody does it sharper, smarter, or with more style."

–Walt Harrington, author of *Intimate Journalism*

"I can recognize the truth in these stories—tales about the darkest possible side of wretched humanity. Sager has obviously spent too much time in flop houses in Laurel Canyon."

–Hunter S. Thompson, author of
Fear and Loathing in Las Vegas

Also by Mike Sager

Hunting Marlon Brando

A True Story

BY MIKE SAGER

Cover design by Stravinski Pierre and Siori Kitajima,
SF AppWorks LLC.
Cover art by Stan Watts from the author's collection.
Interior design by Siori Kitajima, SF AppWorks LLC
SFAppworks.com

Cataloging-in-Publication data for this book
is available from the Library of Congress.
ISBN-13:
Paperback: 978-1-950154-11-1
eBook: 978-1-950154-12-8

Published by The Sager Group LLC
TheSagerGroup.net
In Cooperation with NeoText (NeoTextCorp.com)

Hunting Marlon Brando

A True *Story*

BY MIKE SAGER

For Jay Lovinger

It started out as an exotic magazine assignment: "Go to Tahiti and find Marlon Brando." But the worldwide search for the legendary Method actor, the star of The Godfather, Apocalypse Now, On the Waterfront, *and* Mutiny on the Bounty, *soon became a quest, and finally an obsession.*

From the start it sounded ridiculous: *Go to Tahiti and find Marlon Brando.*

I was sitting in the hot seat across the desk from the new editor of the *Washington Post Magazine.* It was a typical cubicle of a size befitting a section head, located in the far reaches of the newsroom, a one-acre expanse of gray industrial carpeting, spread across three different buildings, on the southwest corner of 15th and L Streets NW, only a few blocks from the White House in Washington, D.C.

This part of the territory was the domain of the Style section and other features departments of the paper. It was known as The Sandbox, a place where movies, food, culture, and fashion prevailed, and writers were left alone to ponder their existential questions and diddle words into melodious prose. Up the several steps into the main building, the more important business of the daily news held sway, presided over by historic figures like Bob Woodward and Ben Bradlee, two living legends who'd together engineered the fall of a crooked presidency, for starters.

The magazine's editor was Jay Lovinger. He was new to the place, a big-time New York guy hired away from the world of glossy magazines I aspired to reach. Everyone said Lovinger was a genius—a sardonic Big Apple native with the distinctive accent common to the region. He wore a silk tie printed with the image of the Mona Lisa, a wry middle finger to the dress code at this august (and always self-important) newsgathering organization, where one was expected to be prepared at all times to be to be dispatched forthwith to interview the president of the United States or other dignitary.

The scene unfolding before me was fairly standard to magazine writers: I was smiling over-large and trying not to seem desperate as I pitched ideas for my next story, mostly gritty stuff that was becoming something of a specialty—a deep look at daily life in a heroin shooting gallery . . . in a run-down housing project . . . at a local gay club, situated just across the street from the headquarters of the Federal Bureau of Investigation, featuring female impersonators and lip-syncing contests every Saturday night.

Lovinger, meanwhile, was staring up at the ceiling. There were no windows in the room. There was nothing on his walls. The harsh fluorescent light glinted off the thick lenses of his glasses in a way that prevented me from seeing the expression in his eyes. He appeared to be counting the little holes in the tiles.

Three years earlier, I'd left my full-time job, as a staff writer with the *Post's* Metro Section, to try my hand at freelancing maga-zine stories. It was a grandiose plan. Everyone thought I was crazy. Leave the newspaper reporters everywhere aspire to join? Give up the golden handcuffs?

But I was only 27 at the time. The *Post* had been my first real job. I'd started at 21 as a copy boy, fresh off an abortive, three-week stint at Georgetown Law. Six years later, I'd upped and quit another prime opportunity, leaving my parents apoplectic and my colleagues shaking their heads in disbelief.

Thus far in my freelance career, I'd written some decent stories for a number of local and national magazines. I had a regular local column. I was making an adequate living. I was moving slowly toward my goal. Then the *Post* announced it was starting a glossy magazine of its own. When one of the sub-editors invited me to pitch, it felt like validation. I knew I was on the right path.

There was only one problem: When you're freelance, nobody gives anything away. In order to get an assignment, I had to come up with a killer idea and sell them on it.

So now here I was, at my big meeting at the new *Post* magazine.

And this famous new editor, imported from New York, about whom everyone raved . . . was staring up at the ceiling. The Mona Lisa on his tie seemed to mock me with that smile of hers, as if to say: *Is this all you've got, Sager?*

I stopped talking and waited for a response. After a few beats, Lovinger sighed and took off his glasses and placed them on the desk between us. He sighed, rubbed his eyes, made some grunting noises, replaced his glasses.

At last he spoke. "Why don't you go to Tahiti and find Marlon Brando?" The tone of his voice was so matter of fact; he could have been asking me to go to the cafeteria to fetch him a cup of coffee.

"F-Find Marlon Brando?" I stuttered. *Is he shitting me?*

"You know, on that island or whatever he has in the South Pacific. I'm pretty sure it's near Tahiti."

"Is Marlon Brando lost?" I asked.

Shrug. Palms up. *What do I know?*

"And what am I supposed to do when I find him?"

"You'll know," he said dismissively.

"I'll know?"

His face darkened. He made this Jewish kind of gesture, something my grandmother might have done. A fey wave of the hand, dismissal.

"Get out of here before I change my mind."

***

I walked the ten blocks home in a daze. I didn't know whether I wanted to celebrate or vomit.

Find Marlon Brando? What kind of fucking assignment is that?

I don't know this Lovinger guy. They say he made his living for years betting on horses and playing poker. Is he fucking with me? Is he gambling with my career?

What happens if I don't find Marlon?

What happens if I do?

One thing I knew about Marlon, even without doing any research: He famously hated the press. And he *absolutely* refused to do interviews.

Even if I do find him, and he agrees to be interviewed, what is he going to say that could possibly be of any value? A celebrity profile. An actor. Aren't those types of interviews always substance-free? What do we expect he'll say to a perfect stranger—a stranger who's only trying to grab headlines and make money for his publication by hunting him down?

What if I fly all that way, spend all that money . . . and come back with nothing?

I could imagine the scorn heaped upon me by the 900 experienced and award-winning newsmen and women who worked at the *Post*, my friends and former colleagues, most of whom were my senior, some of whom I'd asked for advice three years earlier about leaving, none of whom had been asked to fly to Tahiti, on assignment, in winter, all expenses paid, to find Marlon Brando.

If this goes wrong, I will be a laughingstock.

For the rest of the day, and late into the night, I pondered my decision. *Do I sign on for a mission that in all likelihood is doomed to fail?* Twice during my twenties, I'd thrown away sure things to continue on my crucial journey to . . . where? I didn't even know. All I knew was that early one morning, during the spring term of my third year of college, I was on my way across campus to take the LSAT, the standardized test you need to apply to law school, when a simple but drenching conclusion burst over me like a sudden Georgia squall—"I want to be a writer. I want to see how far I can go."

Nine years and counting, one word after the other, one story at a time, I was still on the road. Where I was headed, exactly, I still wasn't sure, but it didn't matter. I was doing the work. I was going there. I was making progress.

And now I get a big shot with this Lovinger guy, everybody's big genius. He wants me to go find Marlon Brando?

What if I say yes?

Am I about to fuck up everything?

As the sun rose, as the first grainy light of dawn began to seep through the slatted blinds on the bay window, as the chatter of starlings and the cooing of pigeons in the eves replaced the clamor and fuss of the dope boys and hookers transacting business on either end of my little street, I snorted the last line and reached a conclusion.

What the fuck?

What the fucking fuck?

There was nothing on my calendar. I had no assignments. Winter was coming—freezing weather, dirty melting snow, exorbitant heating bills. I had nowhere to be for Christmas; I had no date for New Year's or any other time. Not to mention the constant proximity of drugs. Maybe getting out of my fashionably distressed neighborhood for a while wouldn't hurt?

I was 30 years old, divorce pending, no longer the youngest in the room. I was ready to turn the page for the big buildup. You have to dare to be bad in this world of ours, you have to try stuff, you might have to fail. One thing is certain: If you do what you've always done, it's guaranteed to turn out the same. After nearly a decade as a journalist, I'd done a lot of stories, I'd even been on the front page and the front cover. But what had it amounted to? Just so many clips?

It was time to raise my game. To do *more* than just a story. To write something big and important and lasting. Something epic. Something meaningful. Something that would seal my reputation. Change the conversation. Maybe even get me a movie deal.

As it was, Jay Lovinger suggested an all-expenses paid search for Marlon Brando, the most elusive actor of our times.

I took the job.

Wouldn't you?

***

So now I'm in Papeete, the capital of Tahiti. I am hunting for Marlon Brando, walking around in the rain.

It is rain like I've never experienced before: a thick, pulsing mist against a white-gray sky, a tin rhythm on a rusty roof, steady and maddening.

I didn't know it would be raining like this. I mean, I knew I'd be arriving at a time of year that was typically considered monsoon season. But you have to remember, this whole story takes place long before the Internet was created. At that time, it was possible to read a bunch of guidebooks and reference books on a subject and still arrive at a destination knowing very little about life in real time.

I touched down four days ago, flying (economy) from just before dusk at Washington/Dulles until just after dawn at Faa'a. How many hours it took, I cannot say. Across the continent, across the equator, halfway around the world, counterclockwise. Edgy flight attendants, smokey air—there were still smoking sections on planes—a large man reclining his seat into my lap. Time running backward as I flew forward, yesterday arriving tomorrow, brisket and succotash arriving cold.

Since then, everything has taken on the quality of a weird, suffocating, narcotic dream. The air is so humid it's hard to breathe. My bones feel soft. My underwear is damp. I'm looking for a man I'm pretty sure does not want to be found.

I feel like I'm in a movie.

After four days in Papeete, I haven't located Marlon, not exactly, not yet. But there are traces of him everywhere.

Down the street from my hotel, across the Boulevard Pomare, is a bar called Chaplin's. It's named for Charlie Chaplin, who directed Marlon in *A Countess from Hong Kong* (1967). On the wall there is a famous photo of Marlon. He's astride a motorcycle, black leather jacket, Johnny in *The Wild One* (1953).

Marlon is in the bookstore down the street, too. Pieces of his life, anyway. His cultural DNA. On one shelf are eight copies of the classic novel *Mutiny on the Bounty*, by Charles Nordhoff and James Normal Hall, and six copies of *The Arrangement*, by the director Elia Kazan. *Mutiny on the Bounty* has inspired a number of films, including the 1962 version, starring Marlon, the reason he came to Tahiti the first time. Kazan was Marlon's greatest director: *A Streetcar Named Desire* (1951), *On the Waterfront* (1954), and *Viva Zapata!* (1952).

Even in my room, there are signs of Marlon, reminders of him. I turn on the cable TV and find Humphrey Bogart in *The African*

Queen (1951). Bogart won the Oscar for *Queen*, beating out Marlon in *Streetcar*.

Later this evening, *Catch-22* (1970) is airing. Martin Sheen is one of the stars. Sheen is also in *Apocalypse Now* (1979), Francis Ford Coppola's dark epic about the Vietnam War, loosely based on the novel *Heart of Darkness*, written by Joseph Conrad in 1899. In the movie, Sheen plays Captain Benjamin L. Willard, who has been tasked with hunting down and assassinating a rogue special forces officer, Colonel Walter E. Kurtz (after the demigod ivory trader Kurtz in the Conrad novella), who has assembled his own lawless army in Cambodia. Kurtz is played by Marlon.

Everywhere I look, I see signs of Marlon. His pictures, his movies, his legacy. In a way, I guess, I did this to myself, cooked up the mania and smoked it like a drug, inhaled his spirit into my body, his thoughts into my head.

In 1985, when I began working on this story, it wasn't so easy to do research. You couldn't Google movies and articles and download screenplays. Home video players were only just coming into vogue; you could choose Beta Max or VCR. Video stores were starting to pop up in every neighborhood; you left a credit card imprint and they gave you a membership and you could rent so many films at a time.

After I took the Marlon job, the first thing I did was buy a VCR. I was actually one of the first on my street to be able to watch movies at home. Then I went about the difficult task of identifying and collecting every single one of Marlon's 50-odd movies. Then, because there was a time limit on rentals, I bought another VCR. In those days, before anyone was thinking about piracy, you could bootleg anything and get a clear copy to put in your library.

Most of my research was carried out at the Library of Congress, the research library that officially serves the U.S. Congress and the *de facto* national library of the United States. The oldest federal cultural institution in the nation, it is housed in three buildings on Capitol Hill, whch contain research materials from all parts of the world, in more than 450 languages.

This is how it worked: You'd go through the classic, wood and brass, pull-out card files; the large and cumbersome readers' guide to periodicals; the microfiche files; and other available indexes to try to find citations for the books, magazines, and videos you wanted to access.

For example, I found a citation for a much-discussed *New Yorker* profile of Marlon by Truman Capote, published in November, 1957. In order to read it, I filled out a form with all the requested information and handed it to one of the kind librarians, who folded it neatly and placed it into cannister and then into a pneumatic tube and sent it off somewhere, presumably the "stacks," where everything was carefully stored.

Two hours later, the magazine arrived on a rolling cart, pushed by another library worker, along with other people's requests.

Every day, for the next six weeks, I rode my motorcycle to the Library of Congress (despite the cold, it was easier to park). You couldn't remove any materials from the Library. The copy machine took dimes. I had a huge stash of dimes I kept in a tube sock. At that time, Washington was not so safe. It got dark early. I used to joke that the sock would make a great weapon if needed. It never was. Every night, when I got home, I darkened the lights in my living room and thumbed the remote control, and old moments from Hollywood returned. Marlon moved across the screen in many guises, inhabiting first my 24-inch Sony monitor and, later, the screen inside my brain.

He was Napoleon, Fletcher Christian, the Godfather, Julius Caesar, Sky Masterson, Jor-El. Turned-down lips, carved jaw, high cheekbones, almond eyes, tousled hair. A brute, a fop, a dandy, an eyeball in a cave. A statesman, a queer, a killer. A don, a wheelchair-bound vet, a Japanese interpreter, a Nazi officer . . .

I got kind of obsessed; I stopped going out, except to the Library and the various video stores I'd joined. Maybe I was doing too much coke, staying up too many nights without sleep, but I went with it. As an actor, Marlon practiced a form of Stanislavski's Method; I decided it wouldn't be a bad idea to apply it to my reporting. Total immersion. Full gonzo, like Hunter S. Thompson doing *Hells Angels*.

I copied Marlon's pictures and taped them to the walls. I read every article and book available in the most complete library in America. For good measure, as I watched the movies, I sat on the living room floor with my mirror and my clunky "portable" computer, an ancestor to the laptop, and transcribed every line of Marlon's movie dialogue. Stop. Rewind. Play. Pause. Stop. Rewind. Play. Pause.

I dropped down deep, very deep, into my own kind of Method: In one of Marlon's wives I saw an old girlfriend; in his divorces I saw my ex-wife; in his art I found meaning; in his vision I saw purpose, too. I watched a snail crawl along the edge of a straight razor. Crawling, slithering, along the edge of a straight razor . . . and surviving. That was my dream. That was my nightmare. That and the others, gray and half formed, fitful and flickering in the hours before dawn.

One day it hit me: James Dean, Robert De Niro, Paul Newman, Sean Penn—all of them were descendants of Marlon. He was the template for two generations of actors—and for two generations of men. He wore jeans, he did his own thing, he succeeded in what he tried. He was tough and sensitive, gifted and crude. He was talented, he made a lot of money, he believed in doing good works for important causes. He tried to create a small personal utopia on a South Pacific atoll where his own sensibilities could rule. So many little pieces of what we are today are remnants of Marlon; like mercury in the food chain, there are traces of him everywhere. The way he sneers and puts on his sunglasses in *The Wild One*. The way he smells his lapel rose in *The Godfather*. The way he cries for Stella in *Streetcar*. The way he boycotted the Oscars, sending a young Indian woman in his place to refuse the award and talk about Native American rights. Blue jeans and a white undershirt: Marlon. He is in all of us.

In the 1970s, Marlon starred in some of the most iconic films in history. *The Godfather* (1972), *Last Tango in Paris* (1972), *The Missouri Breaks* (1976), and *Apocalypse Now* (1979).

And then, at the height of his fame, he split from the whole program, like a modern-day Robinson Crusoe who'd engineered his own shipwreck.

The more I learned, the more I began to understand, the more I admired him. He was a tough motherfucker, and sensitive too. An original. A true genius who didn't care what anyone said.

I started to think it would actually be an excellent idea to find Marlon Brando and ask him for some guidance on the world's behalf—to ask him what he thinks, where we should be going, what we should be doing, what is supposed to come next.

Look around. Everywhere on the planet things seem so bleak. War. Famine. Disease. Diminishing natural resources. The vanishing middle class. Our sorry excuses for elected leaders. Then as now, things felt pretty dire.

Maybe Marlon has some answers, I figured.

Maybe Marlon can show us the way.

All I needed to do was find him and convince him to talk.

***

After walking around the city in the rain for a few days to get my bearings and shake my jet lag, I figure I'll start my hunt by consulting a local journalist.

The resident colleague is always a good bet for the foreign correspondent, or even a national one. Surely, he or she will know stuff about Marlon—where he lives, where he eats, where he cats around, the usual local flavor.

Before the Internet, reporters had to walk up to strangers and ask questions face to face, and so I do. I ask the woman at the front desk of my hotel the name of the best newspaper in town. Because the phone book is in French, I further ask for help finding an address for the headquarters of *Le Nouveau Journal*.

It isn't far by taxi. Upon arrival, I approach the newspaper's reception desk. Because I speak neither French nor Tahitian, I resort to mime. I type on an imaginary typewriter. I do a Godfather imitation, complete with out-thrust lower jaw.

The receptionist looks at me like I'm from another planet.

Finally, I say the only thing I know how to say in French: "*Parlez-vous anglais?*"

She picks up the phone.

In due course, Dany Weus appears.

Weus is ultra-thin and sunburned, with a pointed face that reminds me of a mongoose. He leads me through a courtyard, up some stairs, into a room with three desks. He sits down and offers me a chair.

I light his cigarette and then one for myself. I lean close and cut to the chase: "I've been sent by the *Washington Post* to find Marlon Brando. You think you could give me any help?"

Weus' eyes bulge. He nearly chokes on his cigarette.

"Watergate!" he coughs. "*Washington Post!* Bob Woodward! You know Bob Woodward?"

He takes out a pad and a pen. "How do you spell your name?" he asks.

I began spelling: M... I... K... and then it hits me.

"*Waitaminute!* Why do you want the spelling of my name?"

"We make the story of you searching for Marlon Brando!" Weus says. He is very excited, still coughing and choking. "We make the picture of you, we do interview!"

Whoa, nellie!

This is not the kind of help I need at this point—Marlon picking up the local newspaper and reading about my hunt for him?

I don't think so.

I smile collegially and and stub my cigarette in the ashtray. Rising, I offer my hand to Weus.

I promise I'll call when I'm further along.

***

In 1946, Marlon dictated the following biography. It appeared in the playbill for his second Broadway play, *Truckline Cafe*.

"Born in Bangkok, Siam, the son of an entomologist now affiliated with the Field Museum in Chicago, Mr. Brando passed his early years in Calcutta, Indochina, the Mongolian Desert, and Ceylon. His formal education began in Switzerland and ended in Minnesota, where he found the rigid restriction of military school too confining. After a period in which he saw himself as a potential tympanic maestro, he came to New York and studied acting."

Since 1950, when he appeared as a paraplegic war vet in *The Men*, the first of his 53 movies, Marlon has done his best to keep his feelings and his personal life private. In the face of his ever-growing success, and the absolute lack of details he was willing to provide, journalists did what they do best when slighted—they made stuff up that was clever and sounded good. He's been called "The Brilliant Brat," "The Walking Hormone Factory," "The Valentino of the Bop Generation," and the "World's Highest-Paid Geek."

Journalists have approached him at parties with lines like, "You seem pretty normal," only to have Marlon walk quietly to a corner and stand on his head. They have talked him into doing interviews, only to have Marlon sit in a faux-catatonic state for 30 minutes, then get up and leave. They've written that Marlon was personally responsible for $6 million of the $21 million cost overrun in the filming of *Mutiny on the Bounty*. They've written that he demanded his lines be written on Maria Schneider's ass during the filming of *Last Tango in Paris*. (The request was turned down by the director. In fact, all of his lines were written on cue cards placed around the set. That's what he's doing when he's looking everywhere but at his scene partner. Somehow, in the film, his bizarre choice seems perfect, his seeming inability to connect helping in the portrayal of his character.)

Journalists have complained that Marlon mumbled instead of enunciating like a proper spittle-throwing actor of the Classical School. That he "phoned-in" performances, tyrannized directors, threw temper tantrums. They have cycled and recycled half-baked mythologies: The time Marlon set his sweater on fire in an elevator of a department store. The time, during the Depression, he brought home a derelict woman he'd met along the road to make a point about his own parents' drinking. The time he stole the clapper from the bell at military school.

Journalists have quoted his grandmother saying, "Bud was always falling for the cross-eyed girls." An unnamed actress was once quoted as punning: "If he's Don Juan, he's done them all." Journalists have uncovered nude paintings of his first fiancée, Josanne Mariani-Berenger, daughter of a French fisherman. They have traveled around the world chasing rumors that his first wife was not, in reality, Anna Kashfi, a Hindu from Calcutta, but rather Joan O'Callaghan, the daughter of a Welsh factory worker.

Journalists updated the public on every new twist in his 14-year court battle over the custody of his son by Kashfi/O'Callaghan; on every new romance; on Rita Moreno's overdose of sleeping pills at his Hollywood home; on a Philippine woman's paternity suit; on Frances Nuyen's inability to play the title role in *The World of Suzie Wong* (1960) on the screen because of her depression after he dumped her. They have called him a genius and a slob. They have written stories headlined: "Brando: An Explosive Young Man's Fight to Be Himself," "Brando—The Real Story," "My Friend Brando," "Idealism Is a Snare for Citizen Brando," "Brando in Search of Himself." Said the *New York Times Magazine*: "Brando's riddled with paradoxes. And conflicts. And inner problems. An extraordinarily complicated Joe trying to understand himself, to come to terms with himself, to uncover his own identity."

In 1977, Marlon agreed to do an extensive interview, in *Playboy's* respected Q & A format, in order to "pay back a debt, so to speak" to the magazine's founder, Hugh Hefner, who several years earlier had posted bond when American Indian Movement leader Russell Means was arrested.

However, after agreeing, Marlon kept the *Playboy* reporter on hold for seventeen months. He canceled three times before they finally met. Similarly, when he was booked on a TV-chat show with the popular host Dick Cavett to promote the movie *Superman* (1978), Marlon talked for ninety minutes about Native American issues—and never once mentioned the movie. During an interview with BBC, he did the same. The interviewer would ask a question on the order of, "Was it difficult to get into your costume for *Superman*?"

And Marlon would answer, "In 1873, Wounded Knee took place. It was a travesty for our nation."

As he would tell *Playboy* when he finally sat for a series of meetings on Teti'aroa: "I've regretted most interviews.

"I'm not going to lay myself at the feet of the American public and invite them into my soul. My soul is a private place," Marlon said. "People believe what they will believe . . . People will like you who never met you . . . and then people also will hate you, for reasons that have nothing to do with any real experience with you. Why should I talk to anyone?"

***

I'm in the Terrace Bar at the Ibis Hotel.

The rain has stopped; the sun pounds the pavement, raising steam. Ants swarm, mosquitoes buzz. I get the feeling that within the hedge row of plants skirting the terrace a savage spirit has awakened, causing buds to form and stalks to shoot and flowers to pop open. The air is very humid, thick with mildew and the perfume of pollen. It is difficult to breathe.

Beyond the hedge, a modern city hunkers beside the concrete docks and the lava rock shoreline. Traffic swirls on streets lined with palm trees, a Third World motor drone of scooter burp and diesel belch and the angry hornet buzz of two stroke engines, all of it mixing in the immediate atmosphere with the smells of rain and earth and flowers, hanging suspended in the viscuos air, pinioned between thick clouds and the high-green mountains flanking the city.

Mini-cars line the narrow streets, side wheels parked on the sidewalks. American retirees off the cruise ship *Liberté* deliberate in small groups, deciding which tour to take. A pimp named Louis—a brown bulldog of a man with thick lips, broad brow, and bowed legs—paces nervously beneath an awning, three packs of cigarettes in one hand, wondering, perhaps, where his workforce has gone. Two men, both of them with a ragged appearance that suggests homelessness, sit together on a public bench, a couple of fishing poles on the ground at their feet. Between them, on a newspaper, a fat, foot-long fish lies on its flank, eye staring upward into infinity. One of the men slices off a red chunk of meat and hands it to the other—a sushi lunch straight from the ocean.

Myself, I'm drinking my zillionth espresso—it is after all a city built and presided over by the French. Papeete's growth was spurred especially by France's decision, in the early 1960s, to locate its nuclear weapons test range on the atolls of Mururoa and Fangataufa, 900 miles to the east of Tahiti. To service their efforts, the French built Faa'a airport, to this day the only international hub in French Polynesia. On the occasions the French conducted nuclear test detonations, spontaneous rioting erupted in the usually sleepy administrative capital in Papeete. The last such test was conducted in the 1990s; Tahiti remains part of the administrative territory of French Polynesia, eternally a reminder of a bygone colonial era.

As part of my research, I'm paging through one of the books I've acquired, entitled *Brando for Breakfast*, written by one of Marlon's ex-wives, Anna Kashfi Brando. Here on page 120, she is also speaking of France, relating the details of the time Marlon fucked a duck in Paris.

According to the book, it happened at Le Canard Bleu, just off Montmartre near Le Sphinx, a famed World War II brothel well known among American GIs for its motto: "You can put what you want where you want it."

As it happens, ducks and other fowl are constructed by nature with a cloaca, a combination vagina and rectum. In a back room of Le Canard Bleu, Kashfi Brando writes, ducks were immobilized in a medieval-looking device, with its head in a guillotine and its rear exposed, at an appropriate height, to the customer, who would introduce his penis and commence thrusting. As the customer approached his climax, he'd signal an attendant and the duck would be decapitated. The death spasms were said to generate "waves of ecstasy."

At least that's what she wrote. The book had been published by an outfit called Berkley. Presumably there were fact checkers?

In later years, with the passage of time and the help of the Internet, I would read many other books and articles about Marlon. Most contained as much speculation as fact, which led me to the conclusion that only one fact about Marlon's inner life or character is entirely undebatable: He didn't want his personal thoughts or history to be made public. (At least until he was nearing his death, when he began to share his secret writings and recordings with the intent of creating a memoir.)

All through his lifetime, Marlon would tell a lot of people a lot of things, much of it fabricated. In his youth, the deception might have been motivated chiefly by insecurity. Later, I think, his motivation became more perverse—he was engaging in an active game of *gotcha* with the fans and the press who found him so endlessly fascinating. And just like the case of his late-life pal, the King of Pop, Michael Jackson—who also assiduously avoided interviews—Marlon's intense desire for privacy had the effect of making the press and the public even *more* curious.

This much is unmistakably true: Marlon Brando Jr. was born on April 3, 1924, in Omaha, Nebraska. His father was Marlon Brando Sr., a traveling salesman for a chemical and feed manufacturer. His mother was Dorothy Julia (nee Pennebaker) Brando, an actress, theater administrator, and homemaker. Marlon was the baby of the family. He had two older sisters, Jocelyn and Frances.

Both parents were problem drinkers. The traumatic events of Marlon's youth would shape a life story as tortured as it is glamorous. "There was this grinding, unstated miasma of anger," Marlon would later say of his family life. One day during Prohibition, when he was six, his parents were drunk and fighting. Marlon gathered all of the empty hooch bottles from around the household and placed them prominently on the front porch for all the neighbors to see.

A few years later, Marlon was riding his bike past a local lake when he came across a woman who was staggering and incoherent, reeking of booze. "I took her home," Marlon would later recall. He told his parents pointedly: "I think we should take care of her because she's sick."

Brando Sr. was a veteran of World War I. In addition to being an alcoholic, he was also a womanizer, the stereotype of a traveling salesman, maintaining casual relationships with different women in different cities along his routes, according to Marlon biographer,

William J. Mann, author of *The Contender*. When Brando Sr. was home, he was physically and emotionally abusive, according to several sources.

"Most of my childhood memories of my father are of being ignored," Marlon would write in his memoir, *Brando: Songs My Mother Taught Me*.

"I was his namesake, but nothing I did ever pleased or even interested him. He enjoyed telling me I couldn't do anything right. He had a habit of telling me I would never amount to anything. He was far more emotionally destructive than he realized. I was never rewarded by him with a comment, a look or a hug. He was a card-carrying prick whose mother deserted him when he was four years old—just disappeared, ran off someplace—and he was shunted from one spinster aunt to another. I think he deeply resented women because of that experience. I loved him and hated him at the same time. He was a frightening, silent, brooding, angry, hard-drinking, rude man, a bully who loved to give orders and issue ultimatums— and he was just as tough as he talked. Perhaps that's why I've had a lifelong aversion to authority. He had reddish, sandy hair, was tall and handsome and had an overwhelming masculine presence. His blood consisted of compounds of alcohol, testosterone, adrenaline and anger. On the other hand, he could make any room fill with laughter. Women found him fetching, strong and handsome. And surprisingly, he had an extraordinary sense of the absurd."

Marlon's mother, known as Dodie, was born in 1897, and would, throughout her lifetime, be described as "unconventional," usually in an unflattering context. She smoked in public, wore pants, drove cars, went to bars and nightspots unescorted. According to the book *Somebody*, by Stefan Kanfer, excerpted in the *New York Times*, Dodie "came from a background of mavericks, gold prospectors, and Christian Scientists. She married at twenty-one but continued to attract whistles and social attention as a vivacious flapper with artistic yearnings."

Early on, Dodie gravitated towards Omaha's bohemian community and toward the theater. She began acting at the Omaha Community Playhouse. From walk-ons and juvenile leads, she progressed to starring parts in *Pygmalion* and *Anna Christie*. Later, Dodie became an administrator of the Playhouse. One summer, she did a friend a favor by casting her college-age son in a play. The kid's name: Henry Fonda. He would go on to become one of Hollywood's greats. Dodie's affair with the younger actor was one of many over the course of her marriage, according to various Marlon biographers, and quotes from Marlon himself.

During the early days of his life in Omaha, according Marlon's sister Frances (known as Franny), Marlon played happily in his grandmother's big backyard on Thirty-Second Street, an idyllic, sunny space with a wisteria arbor. Every morning, bread and milk were delivered by horse-drawn wagons. There were trees to climb, picnics, and adventures with the neighborhood kids.

When Marlon was six, the family moved to Evanston, Ill., so they could be closer to his father's new job as a salesman for the Chicago-based Calcium Carbonate Corporation, which sold chemical products for building and farming.

By this time, "The kid (Marlon) was a total menace," according to an interview of a Brando neighbor by Darwin Porter for his biography *Brando Unzipped.* "The father was always on the road with one of his whores, the mother out drunk in some cheap motor court with someone's husband. That little brat Marlon once dropped my cocker spaniel into my well. I was glad when Omaha saw the last of that brood."

In his new job, during the height of the Great Depression, Brando Sr. was heard to brag that he earned the considerable salary of $1000 a month plus commissions. He was also heard to say many times he considered his job a gift and a privilege. In Evanston, the family lived in a comfortable house on a quiet street lined with green and red maples and flowering crabapple trees. There were four bedrooms, a marble fireplace, and a grassy front lawn.

When Marlon was 12, Dodie left her husband and took the kids to Santa Ana, California. Two years later, they returned to Evanston and reunited with Brando Sr., the first of a number of splits and reconciliations. Despite the bad marriage, there seems to have been the kind of fiery and destructive connection between the couple that summons the image of Stanley and Stella in Tennessee Williams' *A Streetcar Named Desire*, for which Marlon would garner a considerable amount of his early fame—and the first of his four Oscar nominations for best actor.

Upon the couple's reunion, the family moved into a farmhouse. There were chickens and a cow named Violet, which Marlon was tasked with milking twice a day. A cute story from the period has a number of barn cats lined up in a tidy row while Marlon squirts milk expertly from the udder toward each cat in turn.

Other stories about his farm chores are not so charming. Like the time Violet pooped into a full milk bucket Marlon had left in the wrong place and Brando Sr. had a fit. Or the time Brando Sr. insisted Marlon milk Violet after he'd already dressed up in his good clothes for a school dance. Marlon would remember for a lifetime the reek of manure on his good shoes following him around the entire night.

When Marlon was 16, he received a full set of Slingerland drums, which he was allowed to set up in the living room. His idols became the jazz drummers Gene Krupa and Buddy Rich. After Marlon's death, biographer Mann would be given full access to all of Marlon's papers and audio tapes. Mann quotes Marlon as saying, "I would turn the radio up and play my drums for about eight hours." Continues Mann: "Machine-gun drumming—that's what (Marlon) called it, his hands moving so fast over the drums they were a pink blur."

Dodie Brando allowed Marlon to practice his drums whenever he wanted. He'd put on Big Band records and play along. Sometimes Dodie would join in and sing. Whenever Marlon wanted to recall a happy memory of his childhood, Mann writes, "all he had to do was close his eyes and think of his mother playing the piano—'one of the few times we had any family activity,'" Marlon once said. Seated at the piano, Dodie taught Bud and his sisters 'the lyrics and tune of almost every song ever written.' For hours they'd sing all sorts of songs, including popular standards, religious hymns and Old-World lullabies, like 'Annie Laurie' and 'Killarney.'

"But then his father would return home from one of his sales trips," Mann writes, "and the piano cover would be closed, the singing would come to an end, and a black silence would descend over the house. If Bud tried to play the drums when his father was home, he'd be told to 'stop that infernal noise.'"

According to Mann, Marlon demonstrated acting ability from an early age. He was a great mimic "who could absorb the mannerisms of children he played with and display them dramatically while staying in character." A childhood friend recalls Marlon imitating Violet the cow and the horses on the family farm as a way to distract his mother from drinking.

Home life with Dodie was tricky. She could be sober for weeks or months, seemingly happy. Then one day the children would come home and find her still in her housecoat, her hair a mess, slurring her words—manically playing the phonograph and dancing around or despondently slumped in her chair. "She'd put liquor in a small bottle and say it was 'Empirin' (liquid aspirin) for her headaches," Marlon told an interviewer.

When Marlon started driving (and Sr. was away on a trip), it became young Marlon's job to fetch Dodie from various bars in Chicago, where she'd become drunk and unruly. In *Songs My Mother Taught Me*, Marlon writes: "The anguish that her drinking produced was that she preferred getting drunk to caring for us."

Sister Jocelyn (known in the family as Tiddy) was the first to leave home. Like her mom, she decided to pursue an acting career, moving to Manhattan to study at the American Academy of Dramatic Arts—at the time she left, however, Marlon knew nothing of Dodie's history on the stage. For some reason, Dodie chose to keep her theater days a secret from her two younger children. Marlon's other sister, Franny, left home next, bound for college in California, where she studied liberal arts, with an eye on a teaching degree. After a short time, however, Franny changed course and joined her sister in New York, where she began studying art.

Marlon was never a good student. He had trouble sitting still and paying attention in class. He was held back one year. In eleventh grade, after riding his Triumph motorcycle through the corridors of Libertyville High School, he was expelled.

Marlon would call upon his affinity for motorcycles in the 1953 movie *The Wild One*—considered to be the original outlaw biker film. Marlon plays bad-ass biker Johnny Strabler. Sporting a leather jacket, jeans, and a leather cap of a style known today as a "biker cap" or a "Wild One cap," Brando created a look and a persona that inspired everyday citizens and cultural icons for generations to come, including James Dean and Elvis Presley.

In the movie, Marlon meets a wide-eyed local girl, a waitress at the small-town Frank's Café. Drawn to the handsome bad boy, she asks, "What are you rebelling against, Johnny?"

"Whaddaya got?" he answers.

By all accounts, this was Marlon at sixteen.

***

Another day, more rain. I am walking down Boulevard Pomare.

A good journalist knows how to adapt. I've bought myself a pair of rubber flip-flops like everyone else is wearing, and a cheap plastic poncho, emergency orange, and it is keeping me dry enough as I pick my way through the crowds—albeit in the guise of a DayGlo ghost searching for something to haunt, which I suppose you could say is a somewhat macabre translation of my mission statement. As I spirit through the throngs in the harbor, I scan the faces in what I'm hoping is a systematic fashion, keeping my focus at a point just above the heads of the majority of the teeming populous, the natives of which tend to be a little shorter in stature than the average Caucasian. Maybe I'll see Marlon? It could happen. You never know.

Since the encounter at *Le Nouveau Journal*, which almost blew my cover prematurely, I've decided to take a slightly different approach. I don't know why, but I have the feeling that if I just keep walking around the city and looking, making a series of searches radiating outward from my harborside hotel, if I just keep my head on a swivel, my eyes tracking . . . something relevant would pop out at me: A break. A key. A door. Something.

Yesterday I'd headed west and south along the main thorough-fare, the Avenue Du Prince Hinoi. I walked for hours amidst the intermittent downpours. Eventually I returned to the hotel. My arches were killing me from walking all day in flip-flops. I ordered room service and turned on the TV. I don't know if there is always a Marlon Brando film festival playing on one of the available cable channels in Tahiti, this time, *Julius Caesar* (1953) was playing.

The Metro-Goldwyn-Mayer film adaptation of the Shakespeare play was directed by Joseph L. Mankiewicz and produced by John Houseman, both heavyweights in their day. Marlon plays Mark Antony, along with an incredibly star-studded cast including Hollywood legends James Mason as Brutus, John Gielgud as Cassius, Louis Calhern as Julius Caesar, Greer Garson as Calpurnia, and Deborah Kerr as Portia. Given the company, Marlon had been a controversial choice. After *Streetcar*, some in the press had dubbed him "The Mumbler," for his realistic style, which ran counter to the traditions of classic theater.

Once on the set, however, Marlon seemed determined to prove everyone wrong. In fact, his dedication earned him the respect of the revered Gielgud, who complimented the notoriously wayward student for his work ethic. In a review of the movie, the *New York Times* wrote: "Happily, Mr. Brando's diction, which has been guttural and slurred in previous films, is clear and precise in this instance. In him a major talent has emerged."

Later that year, Marlon would receive his third consecutive Oscar nomination for Best Actor, following nominations for *A Streetcar Named Desire* and *Viva Zapata!* He would finally win the following year for *On the Waterfront*.

Now it is I who am on the waterfront, or one block north of the waterfront, anyway, another one of the coincidences following me around like a government minder. I am headed in an easterly direction, scanning the crowd, the storefronts, keeping my eyes sharp, looking for details, for clues, for some fucking idea about what it is I'm going to do next . . . when a poster catches my eye.

It is hanging in the large storefront window of a fancy travel agency, taped to the inside of the glass.

Two feet wide, three feet tall, a staged photo: Three beautiful Tahitian people—two young women and a young man—all of them wearing native dress and standing on a white sand beach beneath a crystal blue sky. They are laughing. Their hands are outstretched, letting go a sea bird, which has just taken flight.

And right above their heads, clear as can be, is this headline:

Visit Hotel Teti'aroa
Marlon Brando's Private Atoll

I stop in the middle of the broad sidewalk, frozen to the pavement like a mime. People jostle past. I gape at the poster. I can't believe what I'm seeing.

Hotel Teti'aroa?

Are you fucking kidding me?

(I suppose if I'd asked at the hotel concierge, they might have told me about the place, but this was the thing—I didn't want to broadcast my mission. And truthfully, it felt pretty idiotic to ask the concierge how to find Marlon Brando. So how could I have known, in this pre-Internet age, he had a resort hotel? There was nothing in the Library of Congress or any travel book to give me a clue.)

Before I'd come, of course, I'd read about Teti'aroa. I knew he *owned* the private atoll. I knew there were 13 different islands within the placid blue waters surrounded by a coral reef rising out of the sea like a security fence around a ritzy community. I had figured I would end up searching for him there. I'd even brainstormed scenarios for my penetration of the atoll and the defenses it was sure to have.

In one version, I hired a speedboat, swam ashore. I had my camera, tape recorder and extra tapes and batteries secured in the waterproof scuba bag I'd bought for this purpose at Hudson Trail Outfitters in Gaithersburg, Maryland. Upon making shore, I figured, I'd sit cross-legged on his beach in a saffron robe (also stored in the pouch), making him curious enough to come out to meet me.

Another plan looked more like a commando raid under a canopy of darkness—same speedboat, black clothes, a systematic search of the islands until I came upon him.

When I bought the waterproof bag, I'd also considered buying one of those bad-ass survival knives they had for sale. (In those days you could put anything in your luggage.) For all I knew, when I found Marlon, he'd be living in a cave up a river with an army of stoned Polynesians guarding the landing with blowguns, like his character in *Apocalypse Now*.

In the movie, before sending Martin Sheen on his mission up the river to find Marlon/Kurtz, the commanding general tells him: "You see, Captain Willard, things get confused out there. Power, ideals, morality . . . there's conflict in every human heart between the rational and the irrational, between good and evil. Every man has got a breaking point. You and I do. Walter Kurtz has reached his. Very obviously he has gone insane."

Now it is I who feel as if I've gone insane.

Marlon Brando is running a tourist trap!

According to the sign in the window, it's only forty miles due north of Papeete.

There are even regular flights.

"Cash, check, or credit card?" asks the travel agent, conveniently in English.

***

Following his expulsion from high school, Marlon told his parents he wanted to pursue a career in music. By this time, he'd formed a jazz band with some of his friends. Dodie thought he had real promise, calling him "musically gifted."

Brando Sr. had other ideas. He said, "a boy as easily distracted as Bud," needed "far more structure" in his chosen career. During their lives together, Sr. and Jr. often were in conflict. Father and son resembled one another in ways Marlon Jr. would later say he cared not to contemplate, including "a lack of constancy and faithfulness."

At last it was decided Marlon should attend Brando Sr.'s alma mater, Shattuck Military Academy, in the sleepy agricultural town of Faribault, Minnesota. Later in life, Marlon would remember his father bragging that winters at Shattuck were "cold as a witch's tit."

According to Marlon's autobiography, upon arrival at Shattuck at age sixteen, he was made to repeat his sophomore year, putting him in a class behind students his own age. "Our teachers were called 'masters,'" Marlon writes. "Their task was to educate and mold us into proper citizens, instilling in us the kind of acquiescence to authority generals have sought to impose on their troops from the beginning of time. The military mind has one aim, to make soldiers react as mechanically as possible. They want the same predictability in a man as they do in a telephone or a machine gun, and they train their soldiers to act as a unit, not as individuals. That's the only way you can run an army. It is only through order, submission to discipline and the exorcising of individuality that you make a good soldier. Many people really enjoy it . . . but it was nauseating to me."

Marlon continues: "I missed my parents, who rarely visited or wrote, but I had a lot of fun at Shattuck along with much anguish and sometimes loneliness. I did my best to tear the school apart and not get caught at it. I wanted to destroy the place. I hated authority and did everything I could to defeat it by resisting it, subverting it, tricking it and outmaneuvering it."

In *Brando Unzipped*—which pays almost encyclopedic attention to chronicling Marlon's prodigious romantic life from an early age—Marlon is described as "a superb long-distance runner, a crack swimmer, and the best football player at the academy. 'He was in better shape than any of us,'" Porter quotes a classmate as saying.

At one point early in his career at Shattuck, Marlon announced his intention to become an actor. To accomplish his goal, according to Porter, he began to read every play written by William Shakespeare. He also joined the Shattuck Players, the school's dramatic society.

The head of the English department was also in charge of the Players. His name was Earle Wagner. Behind his back, students nicknamed him Duke. The exact origin of the nickname has been lost with time. "He was known as 'the gay blade' of campus," Porter writes.

Duke had a two-room apartment in Whipple Hall, the same dorm as Marlon. His place was decorated with "antiques, leatherbound copies of the classics, Oriental carpets, and overstuffed leather chairs. He walked around campus in long, flowing black capes lined in silk in such flamboyant colors as chartreuse and magenta. He was often seen driving around in his highly polished black Packard with his 100-pound English bulldog . . . He'd named the dog 'Lord Byron' after his favorite poet."

According to Porter's research, "the handsome, athletic Marlon and the rather effete acting teacher and aesthete quickly bonded. In between his sports, studies, and meals in the dining hall, Marlon was often locked up with Duke in his private studio."

At this time, says another classmate with whom Porter spoke, Marlon began to learn how to "use his sexuality like a weapon. I think Marlon while still a teenager came to realize that many men in the theater—playwrights, fellow actors, and drama teachers—were homosexual and that they were attracted to him," the classmate said. "Marlon liked to show off his body in front of the other cadets, some of whom were homosexual. He never seemed embarrassed or even conscious of his nudity, yet he was incredibly conscious of it. I know that sounds like a contradiction. He liked to show off his assets . . . he always left the door to his room open, lying in bed completely naked. All of us got to see a lot of Marlon's *wacky* that year whether we wanted to or not . . . He was extraordinarily handsome in those days and had a perfect body."

Marlon was also known to have occasional relationships with girls he met on outings in the town of Faribault, according to Porter's research. "He was so striking. Nobody was unaffected—male or female, old or young. He would come into a room and for a split-second everything would stop," reported a classmate.

For his part, Marlon seemed most devoted to mischief. It was as if he was in a contest with himself to see how many demerits he could amass. Clearly, he *wanted* to be kicked out of Shattuck.

According to Porter and Mann and other sources, Marlon's transgressions were many, the worst of which included a stunt at the White House.

As a member of the school's precision drill team, he'd been given the privilege of traveling to Washington, D.C., by bus to perform in front of President Franklin D. Roosevelt. The night before, Marlon left the hotel, found a drug store and purchased hair dye. The next morning, he presented himself with bright, reddish-orange hair, "a grotesque carrot top," according to Porter. For some reason his superiors allowed him to participate anyway. Of course, his outlandish hair drew the attention of F.D.R. himself. That he was amused was all the more infuriating to the self-important play soldiers who were his adult commanders.

At various times during his tenure at Shattuck, Marlon: Removed all the silverware from the dining room. Stole slabs of Limburger cheese from the school larder and placed the smelly stuff in air ducts of a classroom, forcing the room's evacuation. Shoved paper clips into the door locks of several classrooms to prevent teachers from opening classroom doors. Emptied a chamber pot out of a dorm window onto the heads of three cadets. Spread Vitalis, a hair tonic containing alcohol, along a dorm hallway and down stairs and set it afire.

In *Songs My Mother Taught Me*, Marlon describes with great relish the time he climbed to the top of Shumway Hall Tower, the centerpiece of campus, to silence the bell that rang every fifteen minutes, 24 hours a day. "It was the voice of authority and I hated it," Marlon writes.

"At some point I decided I simply couldn't bear it any longer and climbed into the tower late one night—an act that alone made me subject to immediate dismissal—intending to sabotage the mechanism that made the bell ring. But I discovered that the only way I could silence the bell was to steal the clapper; it must have weighed 150 pounds, but I decided to take it. I waited until the bell tolled at the quarter hour, nearly deafening myself, leaned over, unhooked the clapper, hoisted it on my shoulders and made my way down the stairs to the ground. It was spring, the night was flooded with moonlight and I felt glorious. I lugged the clapper a couple of hundred yards and buried it, where it is to this day. Anybody with a metal detector could find it. As I covered the clapper in the grave I'd dug for it, I smirked and chuckled in a way that only an adolescent could smirk and chuckle. The next morning the school was wonderfully quiet. The masters gathered outside the tower, looked up, shook their heads and tried to figure out what had happened. I could hardly contain my laughter at everyone's bewilderment. It was wartime, and every ounce of metal was needed for tanks, guns and airplanes, which meant they couldn't replace the clapper—good news for me, but a crisis for the staff, because the masters had always relied on the bell to order cadets to their classes and other events."

In order to cover his guilt, Marlon says, "I promptly announced I was forming an ad hoc committee of cadets to conduct its own investigation of the crime, which I called a sacrilegious assault on one of the most hallowed traditions of Shattuck. Of course, the staff loved me for this. Then I named all my enemies—cadets I didn't like—as probable conspirators in the theft."

On another occasion, Marlon and a fellow cadet ran off to Chicago. Upon their return, he bragged to classmates that he'd had sex with seven prostitutes, two of whom he said serviced him for free "just to get some fresh, young meat for a change."

Marlon's final prank at Shattuck also involved hair dye: He convinced eight other cadets—all impressionable freshmen—to show up in the dining hall with green hair. "It wasn't just spring green," a classmate told Porter, "It was fucking *chartreuse*." Later that night, Porter writes, "Marlon invited his green-haired brigade back to his private dorm room where they were caught by a faculty member engaged in an all-male orgy."

According to biographer Mann, Brando was expelled from Shattuck on the basis of his failing grades and his many behavioral demerits. Collaborating Porter's account of the orgy, Mann writes: "The president at Shattuck wanted to suppress evidence of the male orgy, fearing it would adversely affect future enrollment. The scandal was hushed up . . . Today, the official line from Shattuck is that (Marlon's) dismissal was 'a case of the straw that broke the camel's back.'"

Sweetening the intrigue is the opinion of some students interviewed, who have said it was Duke Wagner, the director of the Players, who engineered Marlon's dismissal after Marlon began to reject his private overtures and to be publicly insolent during rehearsals. It is reported in Porter's book that Duke's betrayal of Marlon may have come as a result of jealousy over Marlon's love affair with a fellow student.

Marlon's own account of his expulsion was much different. He says the last straw was an incident of insubordinate smart-assery on a field maneuver. "We can't put up with you anymore," Marlon quotes a Shattuck official as telling him.

"Sadly I went from room to room saying goodbye to all my friends. When I got to Duke, he surprised me by saying, 'Don't worry, Marlon, everything will be all right. I know the world is going to hear from you.' I'll never forget his words. My eyes suddenly filled with tears as he embraced me. I put my head on his shoulder and couldn't stop sobbing. I hadn't realized that I had been holding back a desire to be loved and reaffirmed. I guess I didn't even realize it then. It was the only time anyone had ever been so loving and so directly encouraging and concerned about me. I looked into Duke's eyes and saw that he really meant it. Even now, as I recall that moment, I am moved and touched by how much he meant to me."

Upon his dismissal, Marlon was made to pack up his belongings and was placed on a train back to Libertyville, Ill. The cadets who accompanied him to the station remember his "solemnness," according to Mann.

In *Songs My Mother Taught Me*, the title of which references his most treasured memory—the family sing-alongs around the piano in his father's absence—Marlon writes of a trove of letters he'd written home from Shattuck, saved by his sister Frannie and re-discovered later in life.

"I look at these letters and I am struck by the innocence, naïveté and dishonesty expressed by their author. I see an eager, lonely child who never had much of a childhood, who needed affection and assurance and lied to his parents in the hope that something he might say would make them want to love him. He was a boy with little faith in himself, a child who hungered for their approval and would do anything to get it. He told them constantly how much he loved them, hoping his words would persuade them to tell him that they loved him, and he always wrote that everything was okay when of course it wasn't. But these were not conscious feelings; at the time

I had no idea why I was troubled. Now I realize that by then any hope I'd ever had of receiving love or support from my parents was probably moribund."

When he arrived home, Marlon remembers, Brando Sr. was "mad as hell." As penance, Marlon was ordered to find a job. He landed with a small construction company, building houses. He dug trenches, laid pipe, set tile, and generally helped out as a laborer. The pay was $35 a week. "For the first time in my life, I had money in my jeans that I had earned myself. I can still taste that first beer I bought with my own paycheck," Marlon writes in *Songs My Mother Taught Me*.

As the summer wore on, Mann writes, quoting Marlon's private recordings and journals, Marlon began to despair. "Every night when he went home, dirty and sweaty, mud crusting his eyelashes and caked under his fingernails, he could see the hopelessness and disappointment" in his parents' eyes. He'd become accustomed to that look over the years. But he knew he couldn't take it any longer. "It was time, he realized, to leave home," Mann writes.

Say what you want about Marlon—nobody doubted his raw talent as an actor. When Marlon had first begun his theater career at Shattuck, the Brandos were invited by Duke Wagner to travel to Shattuck and attend a performance. Dodie made the journey herself; she was surprised and impressed with her son's work in a one-act play, *A Message from Khufu*—"a rather difficult role," according to Duke Wagner, who told her Marlon stood out from the others.

After the show, Dodie and Marlon took a stroll around campus. She told him she was proud. And she said if he wanted to be a really good actor, he needed to buckle down and spend many years developing his craft. For some reason, she did not tell Marlon of her own past as an actor and theater administrator. When she returned home from her visit, Dodie raved about his performance. "It's the stage for him. I know he'll succeed where I failed," she told family, according to Porter.

After her brother's expulsion from Shattuck, Jocelyn, who was herself pursuing an acting career in New York, made the case to her father that a drama school was the best choice for Marlon. He'd never shown much aptitude for anything other than sports, she argued, and his knee injury, suffered playing football, ruled out an athletic career—on the bright side, the knee earned him a draft status of 4F (as had his near-sightedness, according to Porter). Why not let Marlon take a chance on the thing at which he clearly excelled?

Jocelyn had just finished her first year at the American Academy of Dramatic Arts. For Marlon, however, Jocelyn recommended another program: The Dramatic Workshop at the New School for Social Research, presided over by the great German director, Erwin Piscator. Given Marlon's disinclination for sitting still and studying, Jocelyn believed the more free-form workshop would be a perfect fit. An ad in the Yellow Pages from the time promised: "Perform while you learn! You can get professional training and a chance to perform before the critics and talent scouts."

Unlike traditional acting schools, the Dramatic Workshop stressed performance over classroom lectures and memorization of classic works. Even so, Jocelyn assured her father, according to family papers made available to author Mann, Marlon would be kept "very, very busy" at school. Everyone in the family agreed it was a must.

Brando Sr.'s reaction was typical for him: "The theater? That's for faggots! It's not man's work. Just take a look at yourself in the mirror and ask yourself if someone would pay good money to see a shit-kicking Nebraska boy like you emote on the stage."

But as was often the case in this family of women, Brando Sr. was overruled. In the end he agreed to cover a major part of Marlon's living expenses and all of his tuition, $500 for the first year, paid in three installments.

A few days before he left for New York, Jocelyn revealed to Marlon, during a rare and expensive telephone call from New York, Dodie's past as an actress of some promise. Being the eldest child, five years older than her brother, she remembered seeing Dodie perform at the Omaha Community Playhouse and thought she was "very good." After the move to Evanston, Jocelyn told Marlon, Dodie stopped acting. She said she believed "the light inside her had dimmed," according to Mann.

Typical of his entire childhood, Marlon left home feeling more betrayed than encouraged by the revelation of this family secret.

The year was 1942. He was 18.

***

Benji's in exile.

He used to be a captain in the Philippine army. His uncle was a general. The general didn't get along with former dictator Ferdinand Marcos, so the whole family had to flee to Tahiti.

Or so he says.

These days the general runs a grocery. Benji works as the concierge at the Ibis Hotel. He arranges for hired cars, recommends restaurants, chats up American women and sends them on the Circle Island tour to see the Blowhole of Arahoho.

"Whatever you need," he tells me, bowing his head formally, "I am at your service." His hair is combed back from his high forehead, shiny with Brilliantine. A moustache the thickness of a fine felt-tip marker traces his top lip.

"I am a journalist on assignment," I tell him, keeping it simple—the less said, I figure, the better. "I need to go to Marlon Brando's atoll."

"Yes, of course, this can be arranged." He pulls an appointment book out of the top drawer of his fancy antique desk.

"I already have a reservation," I further explain. "But I need a translator to go with me. Someone who speaks English, French, and Tahitian. I am willing to pay all expenses plus a fee. And they must be ready to travel right away."

Benji leans back deeply in his swivel chair, surveys the lobby of the hotel, over which he presides six days and five nights a week. "And for this *someone* who speaks English, French, and Tahitian," Benji asks, his pearly smile turning into a leer, "you want *girl* or *boy*? Or lady boy?" he hastens to add.

He thinks I'm some kind of sex tourist?

In fact, Tahiti (and to a greater extent Bora Bora) has long been known for sex tourism, a great bit of it directed toward the Polynesian traditions that embrace the existence of a third gender, more specifically male to female transgender people; the proper noun used is *Rae-rae*, or *Māhū* (meaning "in the middle). Having spent a few days drinking coffee on the terrace and watching Louis the pimp in action, I've noticed his stable includes a mixture. If I had to judge, I'd say the trans women were better dressed.

I can't help noticing that the women of Tahiti—Rae-rae and cisgender—seem to live up to their worldwide reputation for beauty. The fact is, it's been at least nine months since I was intimate in any way with anyone. Prior to that, I was married for three months, a somewhat serendipitous (and obviously ill-considered) decision made while vacationing in the British Virgin Islands. (Lesson: Don't go on vacation with the intent of staying sober the whole time. You get bored.)

At the moment, of course, none of that is front and center in my mind. I'm sitting across from Benji as a deputized member of one of the greatest newspapers in the world. I need help accomplishing my mission—I figure I can worry about getting laid once I find Marlon. Maybe he has hangers-on: groupies, acolytes, would-be starlets.

I take a moment to consider Benji's question: what kind of translator would be best for this particular job.

"Probably a *woman*, don't you think?"

Benji arches an eyebrow, also carefully manicured.

I feel compelled to explain further: "When I go to Marlon's island, the people there will have *no idea* I'm a reporter, at least not at first. That's the plan. So . . . if I go *with* a woman it would be a better cover, right? You know, me there with a woman. Like we're a couple. We're on *vacation*."

I hasten to add, "I've already arranged for *separate* accommodations for whomever we choose."

"I understand."

"Probably it wouldn't hurt to have a *beautiful* woman?" I continue, spitballing. "I mean, Marlon Brando loves beautiful, exotic women, right? So, when I meet him, if *I'm* with a *beautiful* woman, you know, it's kind of like . . ."

***

Marlon arrived in Manhattan in the late summer of 1943. As suggested by his oldest sister Jocelyn, who was already in the city to study acting, the plan was for him to attend the American Theatre Wing Professional School, part of the Dramatic Workshop at the New School for Social Research on West 12th Street. The actor Walter Matthau, a well-known graduate, was said to have nicknamed the program the "Neurotic Workshop for Sexual Research." In later years, the words "Professional School" would be dropped; the institution would change its name to New School University.

Founded in 1919 as a home for progressive thought, it had, by the 1930s, become a safe haven for artists and intellectuals fleeing the fascist regimes in Italy and Germany. Since the early 1940s, as television and the "moving picture industry" began to blossom and dominate popular culture, the department has produced future super-stars. Among them: Bea Arthur, Harry Belafonte, Shelley Winters, Rod Steiger, Maureen Stapleton, Elaine Stritch and Tennessee Williams.

Though Marlon had agreed enthusiastically to attend the Dramatic Workshop, it was not particularly because he loved acting. What he *really* loved was New York City.

On a visit the previous Christmas to see his sisters, Marlon decided New York was "the most fascinating town in the world," the place he wanted to live "when I start living," according to Mann. The family agreed Marlon would stay initially with his younger sister, Frannie, who was studying art with the Expressionist painter Hans Hofmann.

Frannie was eighteen months older than Marlon. She lived on Patchin Place in Greenwich Village—an unusual gated cul-de-sac hidden off 10th Street between Greenwich Avenue and the Avenue of the Americas (Sixth Avenue), featuring utilitarian, three-story townhouses. In time, the neighborhood would gain some renown as a magnet for writers, including Theodore Dreiser, E. E. Cummings, and Djuna Barnes. More recently, besides being a regular stop on walking tours, the street has morphed into a popular location for psychotherapy offices.

When Marlon arrived and moved into her Greenwich Village apartment, Frannie was still grieving over the death of her lover, a Navy pilot who'd been shot down and killed during World War II, which the U.S. had entered nearly two years earlier.

Frannie's apartment was small; she already had a roommate; the place was overstuffed with easels and canvases. No doubt Marlon's energy was too large for such a space. "She was really quite serious about her work, and brother and sister argued a lot," according to Mann, who also interviewed members of Marlon's family for his book. It was soon decided it would be best if Marlon found a place of his own.

Stopping into the school for the first time to get himself registered, Marlon received an abrupt wakeup call: It turned out he had to actually *audition* before he could be accepted.

"Just what (Marlon's) audition had entailed, he never told anyone—or, if he did, no one would record it anywhere for posterity, and neither would he. But whatever his entrance interview had been like—whatever part he'd read, whatever his teachers' reactions—he had done well enough to be accepted into the school," Mann writes.

The program at the Workshop had been designed by Erwin Piscator, a disciple of Max Reinhardt, an Austrian-born Jew who had once been the most prominent theater director in Germany. Before fleeing the Nazis, Reinhardt had lived in an 18th century rococo castle in Salzburg, which he'd painstakingly restored over two decades. The castle was seized by the Third Reich when Germany annexed Austria in 1938. After a stopover in Britain, Reinhardt emigrated to California and opened the Reinhardt School of the Theatre in Hollywood, on Sunset Boulevard. Later, after the war, the castle was returned to Reinhardt's heirs. The house and grounds would become well known as the home of the Von Trapp family in the classic movie musical *The Sound of Music.*

Building off Reinhardt's work, Piscator himself became one of the more revolutionary forces in contemporary American theater, noted for the type of experimental stagecraft common today, including bare sets and realistic acting (for which Marlon would initially be excoriated by critics and theater purists). The standards and practices taught at the Workshop were a departure from the "classical" style that harkened back to Shakespearian times (and to some extent the Greeks) and still holds a certain gravitas in acting circles.

During Marlon's first term, students focused on the basics: acting, voice, dance, theater history, and performances of the classics. Starting the second term, schedules were more specialized, each tailored to a student's particular interests.

"The dilemma for (Marlon) was that he had no particular interests," writes Mann, who for literary effect, and to reinforce his overall thesis about the hidden true character of his exceedingly complex, contradictory, and perplexing subject, refers to Marlon throughout his book as "Bud," his family's childhood nickname.

According to Mann, Marlon was surprised and overwhelmed by the level of commitment and ability he encountered in classes. "He was painfully aware of how different he was from the others. The faces of his classmates were flush with passion for theory and debate as they discussed the tension between contemporary American theater and Neo-Romantic French drama. (Marlon) had no clue about any of that; nor, he admitted, was he in much of a hurry to learn." Apparently, there had been some truth to the rumors that the extra time Marlon had spent in the apartment of his old theater teacher, Earl "Duke" Wagner, was not occupied by theoretical discussions of the performing arts.

"A great feeling of inadequacy rose within him," Mann writes, based on his study of Marlon's letters and papers. "He was convinced that he didn't know enough to be there, that he was 'dumb and uninformed.' A frequent inability to concentrate in his classes had plagued him in military school. Making matters worse, (Marlon) also suffered from a form of dyslexia, which made reading difficult. Consequently, he'd flunked many of his classes."

Deep within, Mann writes, Marlon carried close a memory of an early teacher telling him, in front of the entire class, that his IQ test had shown he "wasn't very smart." Now, Mann writes, Marlon was fearful his teachers at the Workshop would discover the same thing. As it was, "he didn't even meet the most basic requirement for admission to the Workshop," a high school diploma—he'd been kicked out of Shattuck before graduation. However, at a time before the Internet, it was harder for schools to check on student credentials; someone had to call or write the previous school for information.

Typical of his past behavior, Marlon covered his insecurity by acting out. He fell back on his bad-boy routine: He was insouciant and disrespectful and didn't appear to take the exalted Piscator's classes very seriously; he was absent more often than his classmates. He did, however, seem to very much enjoy the range of ancillary classes offered to help the young actors tune their instruments: yoga, dancing, fencing, voice and speech. According to biographer Porter, Marlon liked to tell people the main reason he was studying acting was to "get fucked from here to Timbuktu."

Behind Piscator's back, Marlon appeared to be pulling the same public shenanigans as he had with Duke Wagner. Childhood friends remember Marlon always had a talent for imitation; among the favorites was his impression of Violet, the family cow. Now Marlon savaged Piscator's Teutonic mannerisms and speech, playing him as Hitler, much to the amusement of the other Workshop students. Another student who was said to do a great Piscator impression was the young Mel Brooks. Later, Brooks used Piscator as a role model for the crazed German playwright in the fictional musical *Springtime for Hitler*, the accidental hit chosen by the crooked producer in his award-winning musical, *The Producers*.

What Marlon and the other young knuckleheads probably didn't know was that Hitler himself had hastened Piscator's exodus from Germany. He was accompanied by his wife (and co-founder of the Dramatic Workshop) Maria Ley Piscator, a remarkable woman who'd earned a doctorate in literature from the Sorbonne in Paris, went on to a theatrical career as a dancer in Berlin and Paris, and later turned to choreography. Ley Piscator helped stage a number of productions with Reinhardt, including his renowned version of *A Midsummer Night's Dream*. Piscator was her third husband. As prominent left-wing political activists—Ley was also a Jew— the couple fled Europe at about the same time as their mentor Reinhardt.

Despite his bad-boy façade, Marlon always showed up for class when a famous speaker was scheduled. To many of America's cultural elite at the time, the New School was the world's foremost center of progressive thinking. Prominent intellectuals and artists were often guest lecturers. Coinciding with Marlon's time at the Workshop were appearances by, among others, the actors Paul Muni and Paul Robeson, and the writers Sinclair Lewis and Bertold Brecht. One afternoon, in Piscator's office, Marlon met Albert Einstein, who had earlier lobbied the U.S. government to grant citizenship to Piscator. In later life, Marlon spoke frequently of his meeting with the great philosopher and mathematician. Marlon liked to joke he had "a great deal in common with Albert . . . We've both fucked Marilyn Monroe, and I think he was a little better at it than I was," Porter reports.

Outside of school, despite the war—or perhaps because of it—the big/little town of New York was enjoying a time of unrivaled status as the cultural capital of the world. Marlon seemed to have a talent for meeting bold-faced names.

One day, having decided to find a new place to grab a meal, he sat down in an empty seat at the counter of a cafeteria on 4th Street and 7th Avenue. The man on his right turned out to be Norman Mailer. To his left was James Baldwin. Over time, a great friendship grew between Marlon and Baldwin, who showed Marlon around the swirling world of Harlem's night spots and jazz clubs; at one point, Porter writes in *Brando Unzipped*, Marlon bribed a musician five dollars to let him sit in on conga drums with the band. Porter also says Baldwin took Marlon to places like the "notorious Mount Morris Baths at 1944 Madison Avenue," a gay bath house frequented by African-Americans.

"From all reports, Baldwin was Marlon's first sexual experience with a black man," Porter writes. High on the list of other famous men he is said to have slept with is Richard Pryor, a fact confirmed by Jennifer Lee Pryor, who was twice married to the actor-comedian. The producer Quincy Jones would later confirm Marlon's affair with Pryor, adding that Marlon also slept with the singer Marvin Gaye. The rumors that Marlon slept with his Workshop classmate, the Caribbean heartthrob and singer Harry Belafonte, seem to be unfounded—by all accounts, they were just good friends.

Over the course of his lifetime, Marlon's liaisons with both sexes would be too numerous to document, though *Brando Unzipped* is a good place to begin. Suffice to say he lived the life of a beautiful young man—with washboard abs and a sculpted chest—who became a worldwide star. By all accounts, he had no compunctions about his bisexuality, even at a time when "alternative lifestyles" were considered deviant—and even illegal. Stories abound of Marlon being seen in the Workshop dressing room wearing women's panties; or lounging around his apartment living room wearing a frock and fuck-me-pumps. One thing is for certain: from an early age, Marlon Brando didn't care what anybody said, at least not outwardly. In modern parlance, Marlon did Marlon.

Besides tuition payments, Brando Sr. also contributed a regular allowance of $90 a month. But New York was expensive. To make extra money, Marlon waited tables in an Italian restaurant on Bleecker Street, worked as an elevator operator at Best's Department Store and as a short-order cook at a "tourist trap" near Times Square, sold lemonade in Central Park, and drove a truck with an outfit out of New Jersey. For a time, he worked for a street vendor on 5th Avenue, for whom, he once said, he was able to assemble fifty tuna fish sandwiches in an hour.

At first, Marlon remained a loner at school. Few took notice of him, according to Mann. "I remember only a shadow of a young man in those early few weeks, always with his hands in his pockets, looking down," one classmate recalled. Another classmate found him "rather superficial . . . with no depth." Marlon felt isolated. "I don't understand life," he wrote in a letter home, "but I am living like mad anyhow." Years later, he would look back and call himself "a naïve kid trying hard to understand the galaxy he had stumbled into and looking for a purpose in life."

Early in his first semester, Marlon bought an old Indian motor-cycle. Though he eventually found an apartment on the same street as the Workshop, there is no record of him driving the bike through the hallways of the Workshop as he had back in high school. He did, however, take to wearing white undershirts—at the time considered "intimate apparael"—as casual wear, with the sleeves rolled up over his biceps. Likewise, he wore denim jeans instead of slacks; jeans had been invented late in the previous century for use by miners and other laborers: At that time, nobody wore them as street attire. Completing his everyday outfit were calf-high boots and the *Wild*

One cap. During an era in which men generally wore sports coats and ties, Marlon must have looked to people like he was dressed for Halloween.

One of Marlon's close classmates was Elaine Stritch, who would be eventually inducted into the American Theater Hall of Fame. She made her professional stage debut in 1944, at the age of 19, and two years later broke into Broadway. Over the next 69 years, the iconic actress appeared in stage plays, musicals, feature films and television series. Most recent in popular memory were her five Emmy Award nominations—and one win—for Outstanding Guest Actress in a Comedy Series, for a recurring role on the popular television show *30 Rock*. Perhaps the best measure of her iconic fame is *The Simpsons* animated character Laney Fontaine, which, like all *Simpsons* portrayals of public figures, both spoofs and honors her.

(Rendered with crayon-yellow skin and brown hair, and only slightly overweight, Marlon is himself featured in two episodes of the Simpsons. He appears both times (somewhat randomly) in thought bubbles over the head of the character Milhouse. In one scene, Milhouse wonders about Marlon's inflated paycheck for his role in *Superman II;* to save paying the actor the agreed-upon 11 percent of gross, he was eventually cut out of the film. In another scene, Milhouse asks himself if Marlon—who would eventually be known more for his corpulence than for his beauty—loved cupcakes.)

Early on, Mann writes, Stritch said she was "'madly in love with (Marlon). I mean, who wouldn't be?' Those soft eyes, that perfectly carved nose, that smile. 'Girls were faking faints in dramatic classes so that he'd pick them up,' Stritch remembers. Finally, (Marlon) was getting noticed. Not for his ideas, his intelligence, or his talent, but for his looks, and for the confident physicality he displayed."

"I was a reasonably attractive young man," Marlon would understate years later, "full of vim, vigor, and sexuality. I was an exotic person for them. I didn't follow any of their rules and they didn't follow any of mine. So, they were fascinated with me and I was fascinated with them, too."

Said Stritch: "This is how he got into things, how he became a part of the clique, so to speak. First one person gets a crush on him, then another, and he knows it, and he feels more at ease, not so much of an outsider."

In later years, according to Mann's research, Marlon would say: "Do you know how I make a friend? Very gently. I circle around and around. Then gradually I come nearer. Then I reach out and touch them—ah, so gently. Then I draw back. Wait a while. Make them wonder. At just the right moment, I move in again. Touch them. Circle. They don't know what's happening. Before they realize it, they're all entangled. I have them."

Sometimes Marlon would take a different tack. He'd stare at a person until they became so uncomfortable they felt compelled to speak to him. "He would sort of look into your eyes and assess you," according to a classmate interviewed by Mann. "You'd wonder, *What's he thinking?*"

One day after Marlon had finished giving some of his classmates rides around the block on his motorcycle, the group was hanging around in front of the school, smoking and cutting up. Stritch remembers Marlon straddling his motorcycle, according to Mann, "telling stories to his classmates—about his exploits with women up in Harlem, perhaps, or his practical jokes at military school."

"He would regale us all," the former classmate remembered. "We all just stood around listening to him, not saying much, just letting him ramble."

But he shared only so much. "While his friends spoke freely of their childhoods," Mann writes, "Marlon was vague about his."

Said Stritch: "We knew there was a lot he didn't say, that was hidden."

***

An hour after I have my sit-down with Benji, Angelina arrives at the Ibis bar. She appears agreeable but understandably wary.

Earlier, when Benji had called her up and handed me the telephone, I'd explained I needed help finding Marlon Brando.

A long beat. And then she said, in her musical French-Tahitian accent, "Marlon Brando: He is lost?"

She shakes my hand tentatively, sits pertly on the edge of her chair at our round cafe table for two, her back straight, her knees and ankles together, angled primly to one side, her purse balanced atop her lap. She wears a flower behind her ear, and a *pareu*, a native length of cloth, tied in such a way around her neck that it resembles a flowing dress. It's kind of an odd choice of clothing for a business meeting. *Maybe she's come straight from the beach?*

Regardless, she wears her pareu with an easy elegance, a languor, a certain, well . . . Benji has done me a solid. This woman is gorgeous. I figure we're about the same age.

I open with pleasant chat, then move into a standard, vanilla, job interview kind of question: "Tell me a little about yourself."

She launches into a tale of woe. She'd learned English at a missionary-run school in New Caledonia, another French territory, where her family moved when she was young, after her father was stricken with gout and could no longer work. Later the family's welcome ran out and they were forced to return to Tahiti. To help support her family, she says, she had to drop out of school. Since then she's been working the front desk in a nearby hotel.

One day, an Italian checked into her hotel. Instantly, he fell in love with her—a deep love that went unrequited—after all she was a proper young woman from a traditional family and still lived at home.

The Italian left Tahiti but soon returned, hoping to win her affections. He stayed in the hotel for several months. Each night, he'd play solitaire in the lobby while she worked her shift behind the desk. Sometimes they talked, sometimes they did not. Once they played gin rummy together. Repeatedly, he asked her to dinner.

Repeatedly, she refused.

Finally, on the eve of his departure, she accepted his invitation. Upon hearing her affirmative response, so long awaited, he broke down and cried.

Touched, she fell instantly in love with him.

He left the next day.

More recently, Angelina continues, she has had "serious gyne-cological surgery" but is recovering nicely. When she is better, the plan goes, her Italian friend will send for her and they'll be married. Thereafter, he has promised, she'll be able to finish her university education in Italy.

Meantime, she needs money. Her family must eat.

So here she is.

I shake my head in sympathy, utter the appropriate noises of commiseration. Processing her tale in real time, my first thought is, *And she's telling this to me why?*

Maybe she's trying to say, in a circumspect fashion, that she's spoken for? Or maybe she's trying to tell me she's out of commission in the love department, so no hanky-panky on this trip, strictly business?

Whatever Angelina's thought process, truly, I don't care. I'm not interested in trying to make a move. I have bigger fish to fry. I have a mission to accomplish, and I will not be deterred. My reputation, my whole future, is at stake. And I need her help.

There is no doubting Angelina's English is very good. She seems intelligent. She speaks French, Tahitian and English. And she's very attractive. Very attractive. Marlon will love her, I'm absolutely positive.

Also, I'm curious to find out what other tricks she can do with that *pareu.*

By way of explaining the job before us, I tell Angelina about my assignment and my resolve. I touch lightly on my months of rigorous background research and trips to the Library of Congress; I forego explaining the whole bit about doing a lot of coke and using Marlon's Method to try to get into my quarry's head. (I had brought a little bit of powder with me to Tahiti but the humidity quickly turned it into a paste with the consistency and color of snot.)

And then I explain, in brief, my plan to fly to Teti'aroa to hunt Marlon Brando. I take several minutes stressing the covert nature of our trip, how we will at first pretend we are tourists—good friends who have opted for *separate* accommodations. Once we survey the situation, I will then make the determination to reveal myself at the proper moment to the proper person or persons.

Or maybe I will just find Marlon somewhere on the atoll (perhaps not even on the same island as the hotel?) and be able to walk up to him casually and explain my mission, the country's need for his help and his opinion, my offer to act as a billboard for his ideals—one million pairs of influential eyeballs every Sunday morning.

By this time, the afternoon begins to wane. The soft light from the setting sun bathes Angelina in velvety hues.

"Can I ask you one last thing?" she asks.

Of course.

"*Why* you are you searching for Marlon Brando?"

I reach into my backpack and retrieve an envelope that contains my official "letter of assignment," typed on honest-to-God *Washington Post* stationery, triple folded as is proper and rather soggy by now, signed by the magazine's honcho, Lovinger. In the style of newspapers of yore, the letter informed the reader that the bearer was officially representing the *Post* on a story assignment regarding Marlon Brando. "Please extend all courtesy due a member of the press," it read. There was no royal seal but the blue letterhead itself was beautifully embossed on 20-pound bond. If you held it up to the light you could see the watermark.

Assuming a flat, gentle, instructive tone, keeping my vocabulary simple, I try to explain about Marlon's career and his movies, and about his influence on the societal construct of manhood, and about his cinematic, political, and humanistic legacy.

I tell her how this whole thing started out as a simple magazine assignment, a way to get myself noticed by big New York magazine editors, and also to shake off the self-doubt of the poor decision-making that had led to my brief first marriage.

Not to mention the simple lure of a free trip to the South Seas during the cold winter back home.

And I tell her how, after all this research I've done, all those hours and hours watching (and transcribing!) his movies, all the miles I've flown . . . this whole mission has become much more than just a story to me. I tell her how I've come to value Marlon Brando as a world leader who can help fix some of the pressing problems facing people all over the world. "He may well be the key to a happy and prosperous future for all people around the world," I hear myself declare.

As I'm speaking—by this point in the day, I've had a number of espressos, so I'm probably being a little, um, *passionate* in my delivery—it's hard to know what she's thinking. The true language of Tahiti, I will come to learn, is a silent one, conveyed with a downcast glance, a lifted chin, a raised eyebrow. I have no clue what's going on inside her head.

I tell her I've got reservations for two at Marlon's luxury resort hotel. I explain again about the separate rooms. I stress that the only thing expected will be *translation* services. I offer U.S. $150 a day plus all she can eat.

"We fly tomorrow," I say gravely. "Are you in?"

***

Of all the people Marlon met (and had sex with) in his early years in New York, Stella Adler would turn out to be the most influential.

In his book *Brando Unzipped*, biographer Darwin Porter paints dramatically the scene of their first encounter in a class at the Workshop, in early October 1943:

Miss Stella Adler made a grand entrance after all her pupils were seated. Barging into the room smoking a cigarette like Bette Davis, she was actually a cross between the devouring screen presence of Barbara Stanwyck and the steel magnolia aura of Margaret Sullavan. Stella was stunningly attired in a mink stole, red dress, and pink, spiked high heels. In all, she was a larger-than-life presence.

In her early forties, she was a beautiful woman with soft blonde hair, steel-blue eyes, and a sharp, aquiline nose that she claimed made her look Jewish.

Sitting in stunned silence, Marlon found her entrance charismatic . . . (He was) immediately captivated by Stella.

Stella Adler had been born on the Lower East Side of New York City. She was the youngest daughter of a Sara and Jacob P. Adler, whose family became known as the Adler acting dynasty of the American Yiddish Theater, which had its start in the Yiddish Theater District and was a significant part of the vibrant ethnic theater scene thriving in New York from the late 19th century until the 1950s, as Jewish immigrants streamed into America from Europe to escape the strife of wars, pogroms, and Nazi genocide. Stella started acting with her family's troupe at age four. All five of her siblings were actors too. In time, Stella would become by far the most famous and influential member of her family.

Adler's second husband was the producer Harold Clurman, a mentee of Stanislavski who went on to become a well-known director, producer, author and critic. As a student at the University of Paris in the early 1920s, he roomed with the composer Aaron Copland, who would be later called "the Dean of American Composers." One of three founders of the Group Theater in New York, Clurman is thought to have made his most lasting mark as a drama critic whose essays for *The New Republic*, *The Nation*, and briefly *New York* are said to have shaped modern American theater, encouraging new styles of production, like the Living Theater, and also championing new playwrights. The *Wall Street Journal* called him "one of the most influential critics in the United States."

Of his estimable wife, Clurman has been quoted as saying: "She was the most sensual of any woman who had ever appeared on the stage."

Following her training in the traditional (and rapidly disappearing) Yiddish Theater, Adler emerged from Clurman's decidedly *non-traditional* Group Theater, an avant-garde troupe guided by the acting principles of Konstantin Stanislavski, of the Moscow Art Theatre. Stanislavski's "system" stressed the notion that an actor's work must come from within themselves. In time, Stanislavski's acolytes would build upon his system to create The Method, a range of training and rehearsal techniques designed to encourage sincere and emotionally expressive performance. Three teachers are said to be most responsible for the success of The Method, which is practiced today, to a greater or lesser extent, by every living actor. Each had a slightly different approach. Lee Strasberg (who would later launch the Actors Studio) concentrated on the psychological aspects.

Sanford Meisner took a more behavioral approach. Adler stressed the sociological aspects, the interactions between the actor and the world around them.

As it happened, the founders of The Method began working together at Clurman's Group Theatre in New York.

The Group had been founded during the Depression by Clurman, Cheryl Crawford, and Strasberg. Playwrights William Saroyan and Clifford Odets came from the Group, as did actor John Garfield. Elia Kazan, who later directed Marlon in *A Streetcar Named Desire*, *Viva Zapata!* and *On the Waterfront*, was also an alum.

The Method was responsible for dramatic changes in the very notion of acting in America and around the world, turning away almost completely from the classical idea of theater performance—stylized and artificial, spittle flying through the air—toward the more raw and realistic portrayals we are accustomed to seeing in today's film and television productions. In the book *Acting: Onstage and Off*, Robert Barton says Adler "established the value of the actor putting himself in the place of the character rather than vice versa . . . More than anyone else, Stella Adler brought into public awareness all the close careful attention to text and analysis Stanislavski endorsed."

Before Adler, Marlon would later explain, "elocution was theatrical, the emotion unfelt. Through Stella, I, along with others, learned to truly experience the in-depth emotion of a character. The motivation came from deep within our souls. After Stella, actors couldn't get away with that shit about putting their hand on their foreheads and sighing in pain to indicate despair, crap like that!"

A few years later, in 1949, Adler founded the Stella Adler Theatre Studio. Over the decades she would coach Judy Garland, Elizabeth Taylor, Lena Horne, Robert De Niro, Elaine Stritch, Martin Sheen, Harvey Keitel, Melanie Griffith, Peter Bogdanovich, Warren Beatty, and many more. Later she would teach at the Yale School of Drama and lead the undergraduate acting program at New York University. In time, Adler would be inducted into the Theater Hall of Fame on Broadway and also get a star on the Hollywood Walk of Fame, evidence of her wide influence.

Adler was passionate and theatrical in everyday life, as if she was always on stage. Her lectures were performance art.

"Stella in front of her class was volatile, often explosive," Porter writes. "At one point, she fell on the floor in a fit of frenzy to illustrate a point in her lecture on Ibsen. She delivered 'sermons' on acting like the most passionate of evangelists warning the faithful about the floodgates of Hell. As if watching a great moment in the theater, her Workshop students were transfixed by her lectures which were more like performances than classroom studies."

"She made us want to be bigger and greater than we are," said former student Shelley Winters. "Above all else, Stella never wanted us to bore an audience. That would be the greatest of all sins."

Of course, in early October 1943, experiencing his first class with Adler at the Dramatic Workshop, Marlon didn't know any of this. Before the moment she walked in, he'd never heard of Adler.

But now he was transfixed.

"I could have fucked her on the spot right in front of the class," he would later report to his sister, Frannie.

There were about twenty students in the class; only three were male. Due to the war, women far outnumbered men everywhere in the country. The football injury to his knee had disqualified him from service in the U.S. military during a period when 50 million young American men were eligible to be drafted to fight in World War II. Ten million were inducted into the military. Marlon had discovered his own draft status back at Shattuck Academy, when he and a few classmates had reported as ordered to register for the draft.

No doubt Stella Adler was in the same position as many women on the home front; everyday life was most notable in the city for its absence of young men. The appearance of such a beautiful man/boy in her assigned room on the first day of classes at the Dramatic Workshop would not go unnoticed.

According to Porter's account, Adler was deep into her lecture/performance when all of a sudden, she came to a full stop. It was as if a director somewhere had yelled "freeze." Everybody in the room was on the edge of their seats: What was she up to now? Porter continues:

All her other students were impeccably dressed, the young men in suits and ties.

(Marlon had) shown up in a red fedora, dirty white T-shirt, thread-bare jeans two sizes too small that showcased his genitals, and a three-day growth of beard.

"Mr. Vagabond," Adler said. "Please stand up. Do you have a name?"

"Marlon Brando!" he said, almost defiantly, as if to challenge her.

"If there's a part for a bum I hear about, I'll recommend that you be cast."

From there, Marlon's relationship with Adler proceeded along the lines of a romantic comedy. After her initial disdain/attraction, Adler changed her tune when Marlon performed his first reading for her.

The specific monologue he chose has been left unreported. But that night, Adler went home and told her husband, Clurman, that Marlon was "going to become the finest young actor on the American stage, far better than John Garfield."

Garfield was a hugely popular actor at the time, and another alumnus of the Group. Born Jacob Garfinkle, on Rivington Street on the Lower East Side, Garfield became known for his portrayal of brooding, rebellious, working-class characters; in those days, such characters were in musicals and were still boyishly handsome. Though Garfield was not a role model for Marlon, in the sense that Marlon didn't study him or particularly know who he was, his more raw portrayals are seen as a precursor of Marlon's "type." Garfield was nominated for the Academy Award for Best Supporting Actor for his first film, *Four Daughters* (1938), a musical with Claude Rains and the singing Lane sisters, and for Best Actor for *Body and Soul* (1947), a film noir sports drama considered to be the earliest landmark boxing movie, a cautionary tale about the lure of money—and how it can derail even a strong common man in his pursuit of success.

Garfield's career effectively ended when he refused to give names of "communist sympathizers" when, in 1951, he was called to testify before the infamous U.S. Congressional House Committee on Un-American Activities (HUAC). Some have alleged the stress of this persecution led to his death one year later, at age 39, from a heart attack. He was later given a star on the Hollywood Walk of Fame.

"Stella was mesmerized by Brando. He, in turn, seemed completely captivated by her. It was a mutual admiration society," Porter quotes a fellow Adler student saying.

In later years, Adler would say of Marlon, "I knew he was a primitive genius. He was completely untrained, totally inexperienced, a vagabond who'd drifted in from the American plains—but one of such visible magnetism I was physically aroused by his presence . . . Marlon looked as if he might hump you at any moment like a beast in the field, and you knew you wouldn't resist. I predicted that women would swoon when he came out on the stage. I was one of the first among my peers to recognize his potent image as a male sex symbol."

Porter writes: "Much to the annoyance of her husband, Marlon began appearing at the Adler apartment every night. Ostensibly, Stella had first brought Marlon home to meet Ellen, her teenage daughter by her first husband, but Marlon's interest seemed almost entirely focused on the mother, even though he later dated Ellen, presumably having an affair with both."

Robert Lewis, another one of the founders of the Actors Studio, says he went to Adler's one night to drop off a script and encountered Marlon and his teacher, alone in her apartment. "Marlon was stripped except for a pair of boxer underwear. He was sitting at Stella's feet, not having much to say but staring at her intently. She was smoking a cigarette while sprawled on the sofa in her nightgown. I just assumed they'd had sex earlier. I don't know where her daughter or husband were."

Noting Lewis' shock at seeing Marlon in her house, Adler explained: "Marlon and I are studying. Tonight, I'm going to be a tasty overripe piece of cheese, and he's going to be a very hungry rat."

According to the great actor Burgess Meredith, Adler called Marlon "my puppy." In return, Marlon called Adler "Mother Earth." Either way, it was Adler, according to Porter, "who fed the small flame of his desire to act until it became a bonfire."

Of course, Marlon's friendship with Adler opened doors all over town. Soon he was hanging out with the likes of the actor Lee J. Cobb, the writer Irwin Shaw, Copland, and more. Meanwhile, at the Workshop, he began appearing in school productions directed by Piscator, starting with George Bernard Shaw's *Saint Joan*.

The Shaw play was followed by three more Piscator productions, two of them based on works by Leo Tolstoy. Ambitiously, the teacher had condensed *War and Peace* into a stage drama lasting three hours. Shortly thereafter, Piscator adapted Tolstoy's *The Power of Darkness*, and cast Marlon, too. Marlon also appeared in an English-speaking version of *Doctor Sganarelle*, a play by Molière. A critic wrote: "Marlon Brando is an actor worth watching."

Showing he was versatile, Marlon also played the selfish twin brother Sebastian in Shakespeare's *Twelfth Night*. In *Bobino*, written by Stanley Kauffman, who eventually became better known as a theater critic, Marlon played a giraffe.

By this time, Marlon's mom, Dodie Brando, had left Brando Sr. again and joined her children in New York. She rented a ten-room apartment on West End Avenue in the Seventies and invited all of her children to move in with her. Along with the crowd was a new addition, Tiddy's first born, Gahan. As time went on, Dodie also welcomed other struggling actors, taking on the role of a diva-like mother hen. The place had the feeling "of a crash pad," according to Porter.

One of the first visitors to the apartment was Lewis. He told biographer Porter the apartment was sparsely decorated with furniture Lewis suspected had been liberated from a junkyard. "People dropped in at all times of the day and night . . . Often they slept on her living room floor," Lewis said. "And yes, fornicated there as well. I met all sorts of people, including a woman who I think later became the wife of J.D. Salinger. Back in those days they called us bohemians, and the word stuck around for a long time until Gore Vidal told us it was no longer fashionable to use it."

Dodie Brando said she was in town to rededicate herself to acting, but it seemed like the thing she was most dedicated to was drinking. Sometimes, however, she gave dramatic readings to the assembled. "Even drunk, she put on a good show for the young actors who flocked around her . . . and she was very good," Lewis said.

According to Porter, New York brought out the worst in Marlon's mother. "One time," said Lewis, Marlon "found her drunk on the street and had to carry her home and up the steps like a slab of beef." According to Lewis, it was rumored at the time Dodie had been "repeatedly gang-banged by an untold number of sailors until Marlon somehow found out about her whereabouts and went to rescue her." Writes Porter: "Marlon himself told (Lewis) that one morning he discovered his mother in bed with a discharged Army man who'd lost one leg and one arm on the battlefields of Europe."

"She promised to stay sober, but she couldn't manage it," Marlon writes in his autobiography. "Before long it was like Libertyville and Evanston all over again. She hid bottles under her bed and in the kitchen cabinets and started disappearing again. We tried to get her to stop, and sometimes she did for a few weeks, but then she would go on another bender. For us it was an emotional seesaw."

Amidst the chaos, Marlon's talent continued to shine. Though he gained a reputation for mumbling and wearing dirty clothes and having a bit of body odor, he was picked up by an agent, who sent him out on an audition for *I Remember Mama*. The part was Nels, a 15-year-old. The producers were the already-legendary team of Richard Rodgers and Oscar Hammerstein II. It was their first nonmusical production after the huge success of their instant classic *Oklahoma!*

Marlon picked up a copy of the script and took it home to the apartment. With all three siblings gathered around her in the living room, Dodie read the play aloud, from cover to cover. According to Porter, Marlon remembered falling asleep before the first act was even finished.

"This is the dullest play I've ever read," Dodie Brando concluded. "It's not for you, Bud. Besides, you're too old to play an early teenager."

Stella Adler disagreed. She urged Marlon "to go for it," predicting *I Remember Mama* would become one of the biggest hits of the Broadway season.

Despite his fears about having to read for the great producers—and despite turning in a terrible audition, as he had feared—Marlon was given the role after the director told Rodgers and Hammerstein he'd seen a "spark" in the lad. That the director, according to Porter, was twenty years older and gay did not hurt Marlon's case any either.

The play premiered on Broadway on October 19, 1944, at the Music Box Theatre in New York City. Frannie and Jocelyn both turned up for opening night, as did several of Marlon's girlfriends, including Ellen Adler, as well as several of Marlon's running buddies, including the actor-to-be Wally Cox, whom he'd met during childhood and with whom he'd remain lifelong friends.

Not long after he'd arrived in New York, turning a corner on a downtown street, Marlon almost literally bumped into his boyhood friend from Evanston, Wallace Maynard "Wally" Cox. Cox would eventually become a well-known actor and comedian who appeared in the popular early 1950s television series *Mister Peepers*, as well as several other pioneering shows in the early years of television. The proverbial 90-pound weakling, Cox became famous for playing meek, stumble-bumbling roles, though his range as a character actor won him parts in more than 20 films. He is also remembered as the voice of the animated canine superhero Underdog.

According to the book *Hellraisers: The Life and Inebriated Times of Richard Burton, Richard Harris, Peter O'Toole, and Oliver Reed*, by Robert Sellers, Brando once told a journalist: "If Wally had been a woman, I would have married him and we would have lived happily ever after." Many took this for a reference to a lifelong sexual affair. (Likewise there are rumors of a lifelong affair with Christian Marquand, a French actor, screenwriter and film director born of Spanish and Arab parents, who was often cast as a heartthrob in French films of the 1950s.) Writer Beauregard Houston-Montgomery told Stephen

Saban of The Wow Report, an Internet publication, that while under the influence of marijuana, Marlon had told him Cox had been the love of his life and that he kept a pair of Cox's pajamas framed above his bed. Two of Cox's ex-wives dismissed the suggestion, saying that the love between the men was platonic.

At any rate, after Marlon and Cox met up again, they hung out together frequently. One night, at a party in the Village, the center of New York's bohemian life, Cox met "fellow stringbean," Richard Loving. Cox had been making his living crafting sterling silver jewelry; the two young men decided to work together, hawking their wares on the streets of the Village.

Soon thereafter, Cox introduced his new friend to Frannie. They fell in love "at first sight," according to biographer Porter, and eventually married. Over the years, Loving would become renowned as an artist, working in many media, including silver and enamel. On the night of the premiere of *I Remember Mama*, Loving was also sitting with the group in Marlon's little cheering section.

Notably absent was Dodie Brando. She was later discovered at home, drunk. (Shortly thereafter, she reconciled with Brando Sr. and moved back to Illinois.)

I Remember Mama was an instant hit; lines formed at the box office. While the review in *The New York Times* didn't mention Marlon by name, it was the last time he would be overlooked by the *Times*.

Robert Garland, writing in *The Journal-American*, said, "The Nels of Marlon Brando is, if he doesn't mind me saying so, charming."

Centered around a Norwegian immigrant family in San Francisco early in the 20th century, the play lasted for 713 performances.

Soon after, through Ellen Adler, Marlon would meet and befriend Tennessee Williams, and spend time with him on Cape Cod.

Quoting "pillow talk" between Williams and a later love, Frank Merlo, biographer Porter writes about the romantic liaison between Marlon and Williams. According to Porter, Williams told Merlo he remembered seducing a slightly drunken Marlon as the "tide lapped under the wharf and the hungry seagulls screeched overhead. I managed to extract two offerings from that magnificent tool before I would remove that treasure from my mouth," Merlo quoted Williams as saying.

"I had a vision of myself becoming Mrs. Marlon Brando, living in some rose-covered cottage on the Cape," Williams told Merlo.

Sometime later, Williams cast Marlon in his new play, *A Streetcar Named Desire*.

The play opened at the Ethel Barrymore Theatre on December 3, 1947, starting Jessica Tandy and Marlon, who were virtual unknowns at the time. The cast also included Kim Hunter as Stella and Karl Malden as Mitch.

Under the direction of Elia Kazan, who had also directed the stage play, the movie version of *Streetcar*, starring Vivien Leigh instead of Tandy, premiered in 1951.

It became another huge success for Marlon, the role garnering his first of four *consecutive* Academy Award nominations for Best Actor.

***

Five minutes out of Tahiti, the twin-engine, twelve-seater breaks though the cloud cover, and thereafter the sky is clear, the ocean a vast cloth of wrinkled blue, curved at the horizon. The only other passengers, besides myself and Angelina, are four members of a French film crew who've just wrapped a mini-series version of *Mutiny on the Bounty*.

Twenty minutes later, the plane is making a full circuit of Teti'aroa, Marlon's sunny atoll, twelve islands situated in a Crayola-blue lagoon, encircled by a sun-bleached coral reef. On one of the larger islands, Onetahi, is an air strip—a somewhat rudimentary stretch of packed sand and asphalt scissored like an off-center part through the lush jungle. I could barely contain myself. After so long, so many nights, so much anxiety, I was really almost here. Now all I had to do was find Marlon.

Marlon purchased the lease on Teti'aroa in 1966 from the descendants of Johnston Walter Williams, a Canadian who'd bought the least to the Edenic atoll from the Tahitian royal family in 1904, when he occupied the very powerful position of being the only dentist in Tahiti. In total, the atoll covers about two square miles, with approximately 1,450 acres of land divided into the twelve motus (or islets) of various sizes and shapes. The lagoon, sheltered and defined by the coral reef, is approximately 4.3 miles wide and 98 feet deep at its deepest. Because the reef has no natural opening, access by boat is nearly impossible. Marlon's stewardship of the islands is covered by a 99-year lease, for which he paid $270,000. The lagoon and the reef remain the property of French Polynesia.

Dr. Williams used the island as a residence and a copra plantation. Copra (or khobara) is the dried meat or kernel of the coconut, the fruit of the coconut palm (*Cocos nucifera*). During colonialist times, copra was the go-to crop on South Sea islands, one of the main drivers of first world economic interests in the region. Coconut oil is extracted from copra. It also yields a type of de-fatted and desiccated coconut cake after extraction, which is mainly used as feed for livestock.

In 1970, Brando built the airstrip and a small village on motu Onetahi. (Williams and his wife are buried on motu Rimatuu.) At first, the village became a place for friends, family and scientists studying the atoll's ecology and archaeology. Later, he would found the hotel, presided over by Tarita Teriipaia, who had played his on-screen love in *Mutiny on the Bounty*.

As we start our descent, my feelings run in all directions. Part of me is afraid of what I'll find, what I'll have to do. I know the risks, or imagine I know them.

But the thing I feel the most, much stronger than fear, is the desire to confront him. To be in his presence, to shake his hand. To show my ever-growing appreciation.

The small plane bounces on the pitted runway and judders to a stop. A dozen smiling Tahitians, dressed in *pareus* and Hawaiian shirts, greet the plane.

They unload the cargo, including mail, groceries and sundries, and we grab our bags. An older woman named Simone herds us together and leads a procession to our bungalows, rustic dwellings of ancient design spaced randomly among a forest of coconut, pandanus, breadfruit, and ironwood trees.

The bungalows are set upon concrete slabs and built primarily of coconut logs. There are no windows. The walls of the bungalows are made of woven pandanus fronds and decorated with artfully crafted driftwood sculptures. The furniture is fashioned of coconut wood, cloth, and twine. The sinks are made of authentic giant clam shells. Simone explains there is electricity here, but only at certain times of the day, and only until 10:00 at night. The beds have mosquito netting and ample supplies of green incense coils to burn against the prodigious swarms of bugs. In the days to come it would occur to me that the deeper you get into nature, the more unspoiled, the worse the bugs. Imagine the welts on Adam and Eve.

Angelina and I follow Simone with the rest of the passengers as she gives a little tour. Before we boarded the plane, I'd again explained the plan to Angelina. On the ride over, I'd outlined it once more for good measure: We get to the island, to the hotel. We go to our rooms, lay back, play it cool. Over the first day or so, we figure out the lay of the land. Then we formulate a plan.

Above all, we don't tell anyone what we're doing.

"We don't want to act like journalists because Marlon Brando hates journalists." The key word for this operation: Subtlety.

Now, as Simone leads the small group from bungalow to bungalow—spaced a good bit apart for privacy—our little group dwindles. Angelina and I are last.

We are standing in the clearing between our separate bungalows when Angela starts speaking rapidly to Simone in Tahitian. Nodding toward me in reference, as people do, she says a few more paragraphs. Simone studies me for a beat too long. Then she turns back to Angelina and says something.

They giggle uproariously, sharing a good joke.

When the laughter subsides, Angelina leans her head toward Simone in a confiding manner and says something else.

Simone's smile fades. Her lips turn downward in stony disapproval and she shakes her head *No!* She launches into a long diatribe, the tone of which sounds scolding. Angelina looks mortified.

When she finishes, I address my translator: "What's she saying?" I demand.

"She say Marlon Brando not here."

I look at Angelina with incredulity. *What in the fuck are you doing?*

Her English is good. Surely, she had understood me when I explained the plan at least one of the several times. Who is the journalist here? Who is the boss? Who is paying whom? Clearly her first act had been to outright defy me.

I have no choice but to smile a big smile of non-comprehension. I shrug my shoulders, palms up, *What, me worry?* Even though things haven't exactly started out the way I planned, I do know this: The measure of a person is how they act in a crisis, how they cope when things don't go as envisioned.

After Simone leaves us to enter our respective bungalows, I put down my bag and I walk over to Angelina's.

She stands in the doorway and we have a little chat. Hopefully, I'm reinforcing the idea that she is working for me, that we are a team, and that she needs to follow the goddamn game plan.

Like a couple after a spat, we go our separate ways.

***

Late in the afternoon, Angelina and I find one another at a thatched-roof and driftwood beach bar called Dirty Old Bob's. Four bar stools and a trio of weathered picnic tables provide the seating.

We stand by the bar drinking beers. She is friendly in a business gathering kind of way, which is fine, being as she is my employee and not my date. As the sun falls, we debrief one another. To her credit, she's been getting around a bit and talking to some of the workers; for my part, I skulked around the grounds, hands clasped behind my back in the manner of a country gentleman out for a constitutional.

From what we can tell, the Hotel Teti'aroa has 17 employees; ten children of employees are visiting for the Christmas holidays. The fifteen guest bungalows are rarely occupied all at once. There's a dining room, a gift shop (T-shirts: "Marlon Brando's Private Atoll"), a thatched indoor/outdoor lobby with a TV and a VCR, and of course this bar, situated in a small grove of palm trees no more than 100 feet from the placid shoreline. Dirty Old Bob, I'd heard in Papeete, was a ham radio operator who lived in Honolulu. Early on during his visits to Teti'aroa, Marlon became a ham radio enthusiast; apparently he enjoyed the anonymous contact with others all over the world. Through the years, he and Bob become great pals. There is no evidence they ever met or that Bob knew with whom he was actually speaking.

Angelina and I split off from the bar, go our separate directions. I take a seat at one of the tables with the members of the French cast and crew from *Mutiny*. She sits with some of the off-duty staff and their family members who are drinking beer and joking around, seemingly unaware of the guests. As I will learn in the days to come, there is no division here between guests and staff. We share the facilities. We eat and drink together. If I want a beer, I don't wait for service, I just take one out of the cooler and record the charge in the ledger provided for that purpose. To my great regret, I never purchase one of the "Marlon Brando's Private Atoll" T-shirts—there is a glass case full of them, but never an employee in the gift shop. And it didn't feel right to ask anyone to wait on me. Marlon had created a kind of egalitarian feeling, as if all the jobs at the resort were voluntary.

I excuse myself from the French folks and join Angelina and the staff at their table. To my great relief, my translator smiles warmly, invites me to sit, introduces me all around. This is exactly what I had in mind when I hired her.

The conversation is lively. Angelina translates bits and parts as seems convenient. When she's not translating, I smile a lot and try my best to be chill and agreeable. If you watch people talk, you can pick up a lot from their eyes, tone, and body language. I buy a round of drinks for the table, offer my American menthol cigarettes all around. I begin to learn some of the names and stories.

Grandmere is a stately older woman with a large, gray, Angela Davis-style afro. She comes from Bora Bora. Her main job is to attend to Marlon's needs when he's here. She's been with him for twenty years. She remembers the time she had to take Cheyenne, Marlon's daughter by Tarita—his *Mutiny* co-star and the boss lady of the atoll—to Aspen, Colorado, for a reunion of some of Marlon's other kids. (Ultimately Marlon will father and adopt a total of eleven to thirteen children, depending upon which stories are to be believed, more on which later.) Of Colorado, Grandmere says, according to Angelina, "It was so cold I thought I would die."

When Angelina finishes translating this last part, everyone at the table laughs uproariously, as if it's the first time they'd ever heard the story of her sojourn in the great white north. For the first of many times over my two weeks here, I feel as if I'm participating in something very old and elemental, something warm, something primitive. We are a small population at rest around the tribal fire, which is in this case a picnic table at a beach bar called Dirty Old Bob's.

According to DNA studies, the Polynesian islands are thought to have been first populated first by Southeast Asians, who landed in Papua, New Guinea, at least 6,000 to 8,000 years ago, via Indonesia. Tahiti is thought to have been settled some 3,000 years ago by voyagers from the islands of Tonga and Samoa. Interestingly, linguists believe the Polynesian languages belong to the Austronesian language family, which originated in Taiwan.

Polynesia was first encountered by Westerners in 1521. The Spanish expedition was led by the great Portuguese explorer Ferdinand Magellan. It wasn't until 1767 that Captain Samuel Wallis sailed the British vessel HMS Dolphin into Matavai Bay, just north of the place where Pape'ete is now situated, and claimed the island in the name of King George III.

Thirty years later, the first missionaries arrived; not until the 19th century would the Tahitian language be transcribed. Before then, all tradition was oral—stories and traditions shared around the tribal campfire.

Popi is white-haired and grizzled, a native of New Guinea. He wears a necklace with five large shark teeth around his neck. His real name is John. He was given the name Popi by Christian Devi Brando, Marlon's son by Anna Kashfi. Popi says he and Devi, as he calls him, were working together one day to clear the airstrip of debris when Devi suddenly hugged him and said, "From now on, you're my Popi."

Charles and Suzanna are from Vanuatu. They are first cousins; they live together in love. Suzanna used to be a radio announcer on Vanuatu, but Charles got tired of the work he was doing there, fishing and making copra—the same as his father and grandfather and great-grandfather before him. The couple came to work on Marlon's island five years ago, seeking a better way of life. Suzanna is the hostess at dinner. Charles does odd jobs with the other men. They are paid about $500 a month each, they say. Rent is free. A small amount is taken out of their paychecks for food. They are planning a family. "We want to live here forever," Suzanna tells us.

Matahi is from Morea. He, too, has gray hair, and a belly like a beach ball. He's missing all of his teeth on the top left. He says he is married to an American woman who lives in Papeete. He speaks English, but not so well considering he lived in the San Fernando Valley for twenty years.

Back in 1960, when *Mutiny on the Bounty* was being filmed in Tahiti, Matahi had been hired as a carpenter; he helped build all the sets. After the production concluded, he ended up moving to California and getting married. For a number of years thereafter, he toured the U.S. with a Tahitian song and dance troupe—grass skirts, fire eaters, the whole tourist package. He remembers going to a party once at Marlon's house in Hollywood.

"There was no address on the invitation paper," Matahi says. "The instructions say drive here and here and follow *pareaus* hung on bamboo poles. They have *soooo* many many poles," he exclaims. Everyone laughs.

The queen lady of the island is not in sight. Tarita spends half her time on Teti'aroa, the other half in a house Marlon built in Papeete. Marlon also has three houses in Bora Bora, where Tarita was born. When she is here on Teti'aroa, Tarita always has a contingent with her from her home island. They take their meals separately and rarely mingle with the guests.

Then there is Teri'i, 23. He got the job on Teti'aroa after meeting Marlon and Tarita's son, Teihotu, in the bar scene in Papeete. Teihotu usually runs the hotel, but he is presently in California, helping Marlon. At twenty-six, Teihotu is roughly the same age as three of Marlon's other sons by different women. Teihotu loves to party and smoke weed, Teri'i says. Teihotu is also a good surfer. He looks a lot like old photos of Marlon, Teri'i says. "He have many girls in the clubs," Teri'i will later tell me. When he's not on the island, Teri'i says, Teihotu goes by his mother's family name, Teriipaia, instead of Brando.

The way we're arranged at the picnic table, Angelina and Teri'i sit across from one another at the opposite end. In time, they fall into animated conversation. I can't help but notice her body language—she's leaning forward and smiling raptly and playing with her hair. Frankly, I can't blame her. He is a specimen—sculpted muscles and chiseled cheekbones, with a parrot tattoo on his shoulder.

As the sun drops lower toward the horizon, Teri'i invites Angelina for a walk on the beach. I tag along—though I'm pretty sure I wasn't really invited. No matter. By this time we all have a pretty good beer and cigarette buzz going and they don't seem to mind.

Teri'i surefoots along the sand like a jungle cat on the prowl. He's like the model of an anatomical man, only with skin; his muscle definition is such that you can see each of his muscles firing as he walks. In one hand he carries his fishing spear, a six-foot length of bamboo with three rusty iron prongs at one end.

A few hundred yards down the beach, he stops, turns, and wades out into the lagoon. For a few long moments he stands perfectly still, studying the tranquil waters. Suddenly, as if throwing a bolt of lightning, he jabs his spear into the water and comes up with what appears to be an old deflated basketball—only it's brown and covered with spines like a porcupine.

Teri'i throws the thing on the sand in front of us and makes a fierce face. He says something in French. He sounds proud.

"He says if you step on this thing, is very bad. Baddest thing in world. It can kill," Angelina says, sounding impressed.

Teri'i turns the thing over with his spear. Tiny transparent appendages wriggle like worms underneath.

"If you step," Angelina translates, "you turn over like this, stick foot on wiggly things. They suck all poison gone."

Teri'i grunts, jabs the thing again, throws it disdainfully into the jungle. Then he takes Angelina by the elbow and bids us onward, gesturing with his free hand like a maitre'd.

The marijuana field is next.

The plants are bushy, waist high. Teri'i picks a bud—fat, green, and sticky. He speaks English: "Is very good! Party! Get big stoned!"

With that, Teri'i drops his spear to the ground and jumps onto the curved bough of a coconut tree. Effortlessly, he climbs the twenty-five feet to the top, where he frees a trio of green coconuts; one at a time they drop to the sand with a *thud*.

Returning to terra firma, Teri'i uses a rock to crack open one of the nuts. He presents Angelina with the tender meat from the inside. She is pleased. He also gives me a taste. It is *wonderful*. Usually, I don't like coconut—I've known it only as the shredded stuff they put on cakes. But *this* stuff is amazing.

Buoyed by our obvious approval, Teri'i walks a few feet to a stand of palm trees, kneels down before some green shoots, breaks off a piece. Shucking the outer greens, he displays the inner flesh.

"Heart of palm," Angelina translates. It, too, is utterly fresh and delicious.

On the way back to the bungalow, Angelina stops translating.

She and Teri'i walk together in front of me, talking, their elbows touching casually as they go. I notice they've switched languages. The rolled *r*'s and throaty tones of French have been replaced with the singsong of Tahitian. They seem to have forgotten I'm here. Or maybe Angelina figures she's off the clock at sundown.

I slow down to give them more distance; at the appropriate place I break off from the procession and head back to my bungalow.

I light a few mosquito coils. Without glass in the windows, it's like an aviary for insects in here. I sit in the rough-hewn chair and pick up my copy of *Brando for Breakfast*, intending to continue my research.

But I can't concentrate.

I keep thinking about Teri'i and Angelina. The way their elbows were kissing as they proceeded along the beach in the gathering darkness.

Frankly, I'm a little jealous.

Or resentful.

Or maybe just a little sad.

Here I am, alone, in the most beautiful place on earth. Of course, I'm not aware of it yet, but it is an emotion I will find myself having many times throughout my life. The path I have chosen is a solitary one. It is as it has to be.

I remind myself again. *You are not on a date.* Let Teri'i have her, or vice versa.

Maybe it will help?

Maybe, after seducing my translator, Teri'i will feel an obligation to guide me up the river to Marlon's hideout?

***

Not long after Dodie Brando failed to show for her son's Broadway debut in *I Remember Mama*, Brando Sr. came to New York and persuaded his errant partner to return home to him to reconcile their long but tortured marriage.

With some of his newly accumulating wealth, Marlon bought his parents a ranch in the sand hills of Nebraska, "which my mother called a frozen ocean because in the winter the broad, sweeping plains were glazed with vast sheets of snow and ice," Marlon writes in his 1994 autobiography, *Songs My Mother Taught Me*, named for a poem, by the Czech poet Adolf Heyduk, which was first put to music for voice and piano in 1880 by the Czech composer Antonín Dvořák. Since the poem was published, the title has since been widely appropriated. Besides Marlon's autobiography, there have been two books of short stories (by Canadian and Japanese writers) and a number of record albums, including one from Australian soprano Joan Sutherland, and another from Lorna Luft, the lesser-known daughter of another tortured Hollywood legend, Judy Garland.

The ranch was near Broken Bow, not far from where Crazy Horse—a Lakota Indian warrior who led the fighting against U.S. government in a failed attempt to stop white settlers from appropriating their lands—was killed while imprisoned by the military.

Dodie named it Penny Poke Farm. (In the old Midwest, a poke was where you kept your money, as in: *a pig in a poke.*)

Marlon writes: "I don't know if my dad gave up the whoremongering that brought so much sadness to my mother's life, but she loved the ranch and the two of them shared a life of sorts, though I never knew its inner dynamics." The couple resolved to get sober; together they attended meetings of Alcoholics Anonymous. Somehow, Marlon writes, his parents "muddled through, taking the shards of their broken lives and fitting them into a sort of mirror that reflected their togetherness and allowed them to live free of alcohol."

In 1954, after ten years back together with her husband, Dodie's health began to decline. Following a trip to Mexico that the couple had hoped would be restorative, they decided to forgo another cold, damp Nebraska winter to spend time in Pasadena, California, visiting her sister, Betty Lindemeyer, with whom Marlon had stayed when he first came to Hollywood to make *The Men.*

While there, according to accounts drawn from Marlon's papers by biographer Mann, Dodie suffered a seizure and was taken to the hospital, where doctors diagnosed her with encephalopathy, a dysfunction of the brain due to hypertension, which was partially attributed to her alcoholism. For years, the family had been worried about Dodie's blood pressure; her mother had died from the condition. Doctors were confident Dodie would improve through medication and diet, so she was released.

By this time, Marlon's eldest sister, Jocelyn, was also living in Los Angeles. She visited every day to help out with her mother.

"Tiddy," as Marlon would call her until the time of his death, was the only one of the three Brando siblings not born in Omaha. Jocelyn was also the only one of the three who witnessed—or even knew about for many years—her mother's work with the Omaha Community Playhouse. Jocelyn's first role on the stage was directed by her mother; around that time Dodie was a principal in the theater group and was having her affair with the much younger Henry Fonda.

Growing up, Jocelyn played the part of mother's deputy; often, during Dodie's bouts with depression and drinking, she took over the job altogether.

"Jocelyn usually ran the show at home. Even though she was only a few years older than Frannie and me, she had to assume the responsibility for bringing us up, for which I owe her a debt of gratitude that is unpayable," Marlon writes. "Although I may have argued more with Frannie than I did with Jocelyn, we were close, too. After all, we shared the same bunk in purgatory. But it was Tiddy who kept the family together. When my mother was missing, I always looked to her for instructions about what to do. She made sure I had something to eat and clean clothes to wear. She was as magnificent, as strong a person as I've ever known."

It is not at all surprising Jocelyn lit out for New York directly after high school. Though there was some resistance, from Brando Sr. in particular, she was right in assuming her mother could not deny her the chance to study the calling she herself had regretfully abandoned.

Jocelyn made her Broadway debut soon after her 22nd birthday, in 1942. The play closed after five performances. Together with her brother, the siblings were among the first fifty founding members of the Actors Studio. Jocelyn studied with Marlon's future director Kazan. Marlon studied with Robert Lewis.

Her next appearance on Broadway came in early 1948, two months after Marlon debuted in his role as Stanley Kowalski in Tennessee Williams' *A Streetcar Named Desire*. Not long after, she joined the cast of *Mister Roberts*, starring Henry Fonda. The play was a smash hit, running for about three years (1,157 performances). Jocelyn played navy nurse Lieutenant Ann Girard, known for "the strawberry birthmark on her ass." History does not record her state of awareness regarding her mother's long-ago spring/summer relationship with the Omaha-born actor, who went on to play the title role on film.

After several more moderate successes on Broadway, Jocelyn came to Hollywood and made her film debut (again playing a female servicemember) in the 1953 war drama, *China Venture*. The famed acting teacher Lee Strassberg, known as "the father of method acting in America," was one of the co-stars. The movie was directed by Don Siegel, a two-time Academy Award-winner known for such movie classics as *The Verdict* (1946), with Sydney Greenstreet and Peter Lorre, *The Invasion of the Body Snatchers* (1956), and the Elvis Presley movie considered to be The King's best, *Flaming Star* (1960). He also had a long professional and personal friendship with Clint Eastwood. Eastwood has often mentioned Siegel as his most important filmmaking mentor.

When Jocelyn first arrived in Los Angeles, two years after Marlon's landmark on-screen performance in *Streetcar*, she gave an interview to *The New York Times*. When asked what advice she'd been given by her famous brother in advance of her screen debut, she said, "Marlon is a sweet fellow, and he works very hard. I asked him for a tip about pictures, and he answered, 'Oh, I just say the words. That's all I know about picture acting.' He probably was smart to let me find my own way."

Jocelyn's second film role brought her the most success. In Fritz Lang's classic film noir, *The Big Heat* (1953), she plays the wife of Glenn Ford's starring detective character. During the filming, Ford was heard to remark that Jocelyn "looked like Marlon in drag." Ford's remark wasn't so much an insult as it was a remark upon the unusual beauty they shared; whatever the problems of the Brando parents, they had certainly made beautiful kids.

Jocelyn's character is killed when she starts the family automobile, which has been rigged with a bomb intended for her husband. The scene, in which the explosion is anticipated and heard but not shown, is considered a landmark moment in filmmaking.

In 1954, during the McCarthy era, when U.S. Sen. Joseph McCarthy was leading his misguided effort to expose an alleged "communist infiltration of America," Jocelyn was accused of lending her support to a communist front group. At the time, hundreds of other Americans were also accused of being communists or communist sympathizers; thousands became the subjects of aggressive investigations and were questioned before government and private industry panels. The primary targets of the witch hunt were government employees, entertainment industry figures, academics, and labor-union activists. Suspicions were often given credence despite inconclusive or questionable evidence; the level of threat posed by a person's real or supposed leftist associations or beliefs were exaggerated. Many people lost their jobs; some had to find new careers; some were imprisoned. Along with uncounted others in Hollywood, Jocelyn was put on an unwritten "blacklist."

Jocelyn eventually regained her footing and enjoyed a modest career on the small screen, appearing in guest roles on scores of television shows, including *Alfred Hitchcock Presents* (1955-65), *Wagon Train* (1957-65), *Little House on the Prairie* (1974-83), and the prime-time potboiler *Dallas* (1978-91). In the early 1970s she had a recurring role on the daytime TV soap opera *Love of Life* (1951-80). She also played parts in a dozen films, including supporting roles in two of Marlon's, *The Ugly American* (1963) and *The Chase* (1966).

Jocelyn's most memorable of many small movie roles would come later—in the classic *Mommie Dearest* (1981), based on a book by the daughter of the mercurial actress Joan Crawford. In the movie, Faye Dunaway plays Crawford. Jocelyn plays Barbara Bennett, a reporter who has come to the great but disturbed actress' mansion for an interview.

Another actress who worked on the film, Rutanya Alda, wrote about her experiences on the set in the book *The Mommie Dearest Diary: Carol Ann Tells All*. Alda played the part of Carol Ann, Crawford's long-suffering assistant. In the book, Alda recounts that Dunaway, perhaps channeling her character too well, was "out of control" when filming the famous scene in which Crawford goes ballistic and attacks her daughter, Christina, for interrupting the interview with Jocelyn's character. According to the book, during the scene, Alda was hit hard in the chest and knocked over several times. According to Alda, the script called for Jocelyn's character to assist Alda's character in pulling Crawford off Christina; Jocelyn instead backed away, refusing to participate in the struggle, no doubt for fear of being injured.

"I was always very close to my sisters," Marlon writes, "because we were all scorched, though perhaps in different ways, by the experience of growing up in the furnace that was our family. We each went our own way, but there has always been the love and intimacy that can be shared only by those trying to escape in the same lifeboat. Tiddy probably knows me better than anyone else."

Once back at her sister's house in Pasadena, Dodie's condition slowly deteriorated.

Her eyesight began to fail, she lost control of her bodily functions. Another trip to the hospital brought further bad news: She was suffering from malignant nephrosclerosis, a kidney condition brought on by chronic high blood pressure. Sober for a decade, Dodie was now paying the price for her past. Doctors estimated she'd been suffering from the disease, which causes hardening of the walls of the small arteries and arterioles (small arteries that convey blood from arteries to the even smaller capillaries) of the kidney, for thirty years. They told Brando Sr. to gather the family.

For about a week, as Dodie slipped in and out of a coma, Marlon, his father, and his sisters took turns at Dodie's bedside.

Marlon was with her in the early morning hours of March 31 when she came out of her coma. She reached for his hand.

"I'm not scared," she told her son, "and you don't have to be." Then she drew her last breath.

"After hearing her death rattle," Marlon writes, "I took a lock of her hair, the pillow she died on, and a beautiful aquamarine ring from her finger and walked outside. It was about five a.m. on a spring morning in Pasadena, and it seemed as if everything in nature had been imbued with her spirit: the birds, the leaves, the flowers and especially the wind, all seemed to reflect it. She had given me a love of nature and animals, and the night sky, and a sense of closeness to the earth. I felt she was with me there, outside the hospital, and it helped get me through the loss. She was gone, but I felt she had been transformed into everything that was reflective of nature and was going to be all right. Suddenly I had a vision of a great bird climbing into the sky higher and higher and I heard Ferde Grofé's *Mississippi Suite*. Now I often hear the music and see her in the same way, a majestic bird floating on thermals of warm air, gliding higher and higher past a great stone cliff."

Sometime afterwards, according to the actress Bette Davis and biographer Darwin Porter, Marlon revealed one night to Davis that Dodie had molested him as a young boy.

"Many times she invited me into her bed," he is quoted, in *Brando Unzipped*, as saying to Davis. "I knew it wasn't right, but I didn't know how to stop it. Actually, one part of me didn't want her to stop. I guess I was in love with her. She was always drunk—never sober—when she invited me to her bed."

Fran Brando later revealed she had long suspected her mother of harboring an incestuous feeling "for young Bud."

At the same time he may have been molested by Dodie, Marlon also later revealed, he was having regular liaisons with the 18-year-old Scandinavian girl who'd taken a position as the Brandos' live-in housekeeper.

***

I wake to a clattering breeze beneath a coconut palm, a melody of fronds like wind chimes.

This is my second day on Marlon's island. It is mid-morning. I was up until 4:00 a.m. reading *Marlon Brando: The Only Contender*, by the same author who wrote *Doug and Mary*; *Lenny, Janis, and Jimi*; and *All the Stars in Heaven*. I'm still a little woozy.

The sand is soft ivory, warm to the touch, with a crust of coral on top—when you walk across an untrod patch, it breaks and crunches as does a deep snow glazed with freezing rain. Red ants skitter here and there, hermit crabs in painted shells motor sideways, probing with their animated claws. At the tree line, the vegetation is lush, a blend of vines and flowers, leaves and fruits. Coconut palms bend gracefully over the water's edge, curved and vain, ripe with green nuts. The lagoon teems with fish, feeding in bands and swirls of aquamarine and amethyst and emerald.

Five feet south of me, on her own beach towel, Angelina is still asleep. She must have joined me here while I was napping. She is topless. Her breasts rise and fall gently with each breath—smooth, tan, tapered in repose. Scraps of lust and poetry float through my mind, and I have an urge to reach out, to touch, to feel the firm softness against my fingertips, the dark thimble of her breeze-beswept nipple . . .

But I cannot, for I am hunting Marlon Brando, and the breasts are those of my translator, a softly sculpted girl of 27 on an ivory beach in a string bikini bottom who speaks fluent English, French, and Tahitian.

And now she is stirring.

I snap my gaze away, search the blue ocean. Sea birds wheel overhead, just like the poster I saw in the travel agency window. A half-mile distant, waves break over the coral reef. I have always had a deep attraction to the beach, the ocean. My parents, too. Since I was young, I've visited beaches all over the world. This one will remain by far the most beautiful, unspoiled place I will ever visit.

Marlon discovered Tahiti in 1960, when he came here to shoot *Mutiny on the Bounty*. Directed by Lewis Milestone, Marlon's *Mutiny* was actually a remake of a 1945 Oscar-winning version starring Clark Gable (which itself was a remake of a 1933 film starring Errol Flynn). More Marlon coincidence: Gable's leading lady in the first *Mutiny*, Movita, became Marlon's second wife.

When Marlon arrived in Tahiti, he was thirty-seven. He'd been making movies for ten years. And he was arguably the biggest star in Hollywood.

After his early success on Broadway in the late 1940s with *I Remember Mama* and *A Streetcar Named Desire*, he came to Los Angeles in 1949 to film *The Men*. To prepare to play the part of a vet injured in WWII, he spent months in a wheelchair. Next came the movie version of *A Streetcar Named Desire* (1951)—with his iconic anguished cry of "*Steeeeelaaaa*" and his culture-branding "wife beater" undershirt—followed by *Viva Zapata!*, *Julius Caesar* (1953), *The Wild One* and *On the Waterfront* (1954), *Desirée* (1954), *Guys and Dolls* (1955), *The Teahouse of the August Moon* (1956), *Sayonara* (1957), *The Young Lions* (1958), *The Fugitive Kind* (1960), and *One-Eyed Jacks* (1961), which became an early model of all that can go wrong on a big-budget film when the star is given too much control.

By the time he got to Tahiti, Marlon had been nominated four times for Oscars and had won once. On the way, he'd inspired a whole new generation of Method actors who drew at least some of their technique from Brando's tentative micro-mannerisms, his realistic choices of diction (mumbling, for instance), and the kind of vulnerable, raw, tender, and sometimes brutal portrayals of reality he was able to bring to the screen. Marlon's acting, taken in context, was revolutionary—a total departure from the prevailing style, which had been borne of stage performance. His looks, his every way of being, screamed *closeup*; he was transfixing, both in person and on the screen.

It is also said—by those who study such things—that Marlon and his acting helped redefine the concepts of masculine sexuality in our culture. Before Brando, the model for American manhood was John Wayne—swaggering, confident, loyal, honest, responsible, unwavering. Marlon played a new kind of hero: conflicted, vulnerable, primitive, flawed. The Method was about realism: gritty, raw, honest. Nobody in real life was like John Wayne.

"Because the typical Brando hero of the early Fifties was ambivalent and emotionally confused," wrote a contributing editor to *Harper's*, "he could not summon the courage and maturity that had formerly been elements of a film hero's virility. Instead, he projected a kind of teenaged eroticism, intense and unfocused, which derived emotional power from an impossible passive yearning. Frustration was the bottom line of his sexuality, the frustration of a man who cannot control his fate."

Complicating Marlon's life and career was Marlon's inability—unwillingness?—to play well with others in the Hollywood sandbox. He was quoted as calling his fellow actors in Los Angeles "funnies in satin Cadillacs" who lived in "a cultural boneyard." He told a young James Dean that Dean was mentally unbalanced and ought to see a shrink. Of Frank Sinatra, Marlon was quoted as saying, "Frank is the kind of guy, when he dies, he's going to heaven and give God a bad time for making him bald."

The two most powerful Hollywood gossip columnists of the day were Louella Parsons and Hedda Hopper. Marlon openly called them "The Fat One" and "The One with the Hat."

Marlon did things the way he wanted to do them. He was among the first to refuse to participate in the exploitive system of studio contract players. He was among the first modern actors to receive a percentage of gross earnings, to have script and casting approval, to start his own production company, to produce and direct his own film.

As is inevitable in so many stories, after the mercurial rise came . . . the weirdness.

By the late 1950s, Marlon's career was not going so well. He made a few clunkers. His newness had worn off; his eccentricities had begun to feel rude and crazy instead of *oh so interesting*. The usual public backlash ensued.

Meanwhile, Marlon's private life was in tatters. He was going through a divorce with second wife, Movita; he'd left her when she was two months pregnant after a brief marriage. He was named in a paternity suit by a Philippine dancer. And his first wife, Anna Kashfi, was still dragging him through court. Reporting on the case, the Associated Press noted that on November 19, 1959, Kashfi "threatened Mr. Brando with a butcher knife and threw a tricycle at him. She says he beat her, threw her to the floor and terrorized her. Each says their violent battles, which included hair pulling and spanking, were the other's faults."

At work on movie sets, Marlon became more and more of a problem. He arrived late to set, tyrannized directors with requests for script changes, wore earplugs during takes to maintain his focus, and gained so much weight during the course of a production that obtuse camera angles had to be employed by the end of filming.

Soon, Marlon was heard talking about giving up acting. He was interested in so many other things, he said. Long before it became popular, he began studying Eastern religions and meditation, traveling to Southeast Asia, and lending his image to political causes.

When MGM came to him in 1960 with the idea for a remake of *Mutiny on the Bounty*, Marlon only took the meeting because he was interested in promoting a film biography of Caryl Chessman, a convicted rapist who had been recently executed in California. On the night Chessman was put to death, Marlon stood outside the walls at San Quentin prison and protested with others.

At a meeting at his Hollywood home with producer Aaron Rosenberg and director Carol Reed, Marlon pitched for two hours.

The men listened . . . and politely declined.

But then Rosenberg proposed an alternative: If Marlon would agree to leave right away for Tahiti to do a remake of *Mutiny on the Bounty*, he'd be given full rein to *personally* cast his Polynesian leading lady.

Marlon took the job.

Wouldn't you?

Marlon first learned about Teti'aroa while scouting filming locations from the air for *Mutiny on the Bounty*, which was shot on Tahiti and neighboring Moorea. Coincidentally, William Bligh, the captain of the *HMS Bounty* (the vessel referenced in the film title), is said to have actually visited the atoll, in 1879, searching for mutineers.

After filming was completed, Brando hired a local fisherman to ferry him to Teti'aroa. He found the atoll "more gorgeous than anything I had anticipated," according to his autobiography.

Half a world away from the cultural boneyard of Hollywood, it was called Teti'aroa.

Tetia means "man standing alone." *Roa* means "far away."

It was perfect.

Before the year was out, it was his.

Now, on the beach, Angelina is waking from her mid-morning nap.

"Sleep well?" I ask nonchalantly, keeping my eyes on the lagoon.

"Yes, thank you."

Her tone is businesslike. In my peripheral vision I can see her re-affixing her bikini top.

"Did you find Marlon Brando yet?" she teases.

"Why you like making fun of me?" I ask. I have taken to speaking more simply, with fewer words, and with a slight Tahitian-French accent. It seems to make conversation easier.

"I not make fun. I just ask question," she says, raising a shy hand to her mouth to cover a giggle.

***

During the adult portion of their lives together, as earlier, Brando Sr. and Jr. were often in conflict. Marlon closely resembled his father in looks and character. Both men shared, Marlon writes, "a lack of constancy and faithfulness."

Despite his frequently expressed "hatred" of his father, and despite the resentment for the cruelties of his upbringing, Marlon seemed to have been softened by his mother's death. Or perhaps he was more comfortable viewing his father as an old man, seemingly broken by the passing of his wife, and by the realities of their stormy life together. In *Songs My Mother Taught Me*, he credits his therapist for helping him let go of the past, though in his writings he is anything but sanguine.

At any rate, not long after Dodie was laid to rest, Marlon hired his father to be the head of his personal film company. Headquartered in Hollywood, it was called Pennebaker Productions, after Dodie's maiden name.

Like many young adults, particularly young celebrities, Marlon relied upon his father to handle his finances. Though Marlon liked the things money could buy, he couldn't be bothered with the details. He felt as if "playing around with money" was debasing, the province of "men in suits."

"Money was never important to me once I'd fed myself, had a place to sleep and had enough to take care of my family and people I loved," Marlon writes in *Songs My Mother Taught Me*. "My father invested it, but like most misers, he was a poor businessman and lost everything, the equivalent today of about $20 million . . . Some of the money was spent on bad investments in cattle, but most was squandered on abandoned gold mines, where a slick salesman had convinced him a fortune was to be made in gold tailings," the byproduct of gold mining, essentially the dregs.

According to Marlon, Pennebaker Productions was founded with three objectives: "to make films that would be a force for good in the world; to create a job for my father that would give him something to do after my mother died; and to cut taxes." According to his father, Marlon writes, "taxes were taking 80 percent of what I earned, and that by forming a corporation we would be able to cut them substantially to put away some money for my retirement."

And just like that, a traveling salesman of chemical products became a Hollywood executive.

The company eventually produced a score of films in the fifties and sixties, including the Brando vehicles *Sayonara*, with Ricardo Montalbán and James Garner; and *The Fugitive Kind*, with Joanne Woodward, Anna Magnani, and Maureen Stapleton. *Bedtime Story* (1964), with David Niven and Shirley Jones, has Niven and Marlon playing two gigolo/scam artists in a Mediterranean resort town who make a wager about their prowess.

With Marlon's star power, he was able to attract other big names to Pennebaker projects, including Paul Newman, Sidney Poitier, Louis Armstrong, James Cagney, Glynis Johns, Gary Cooper, and France Nuyen.

Most notable from Pennebaker was *One-Eyed Jacks*, which one critic called: "a strange, tumid, engrossing Western." It was the only movie in which Marlon both directed and starred. Originally, the great Stanley Kubrick had been signed to direct. Complaining about the disarray of the screenplay, however, he eventually left the production to direct *Spartacus*. (Another dropout was the original co-screenwriter, film legend Sam Peckinpah. The script was based on *The Authentic Death of Hendry Jones*, a 1956 novel, and went through many permutations.)

Marlon writes that after Kubrick decamped, the script was sent to several others, including Elia Kazan, the director most closely associated with Marlon's biggest successes.

"No one wanted to do it," Marlon writes, "so I had to direct it myself. We shot most of it at Big Sur and on the Monterey peninsula, where I slept with many pretty women and had a lot of laughs."

In her 2001 biography, *Marlon Brando*, Patricia Bosworth writes that *One-Eyed Jacks*, which also featured *Streetcar* co-star Karl Malden, "probably contains the most accurate on-screen portrait of Brando at the time, a man with an unforgettable face about to spoil and grow fat, a man seemingly incapable or unwilling to project love or desire to anyone else on the screen."

A few years after Dodie's death, Brando Sr. remarried. At age 70, according to Marlon, Brando Sr. cheated on his second wife, engaging in an affair with one of the secretaries at Pennebaker.

"My father changed little as he grew older; always handsome, always a miser, always a charmer, always a philanderer," Marlon writes. "He never lost the shyness that people, especially women, liked about him. It was something he came by naturally. Though he was very masculine, he also had a gentleness, humility and quietness that people liked, along with a very genuine sense of humor."

Time passed. Movies were made. Marlon was becoming more and more politically active, and more difficult to work with. Brando Sr., motivated by a salesman's instinct for the bottom line, often worked at cross-purpose with Marlon's wishes.

Then one day, without consulting his son, Brando Sr. fired an employee Marlon both liked and believed to be essential.

Already Brando Sr. was on thin ice. He'd lost a ton on the gold mines. The cattle investments had landed them in court. "Due to the old man's blunderings," according to Mann, "the cattle operation finally collapsed under the weight of conspiracy, mismanagement and fraud."

At this point, Marlon was 33. Despite his rationalizations, he was still dependent upon his father.

Originally, Marlon believed that by making the old man his employee, he'd get to call the shots—a testament perhaps to his naive, though principled, underestimation of the power of "the men in suits." As it worked out, however, daddy still controlled the purse strings. Marlon Brando, superstar actor, head of his own production company, was receiving an allowance of $200 a month to cover his living expenses. At the same time, according to Mann, his father's second wife was receiving $5,000 a month. Brando's father also supervised Marlon's payments to the mothers of Marlon's two infant sons—Christian Devi Brando with Anna Kashfi and Miko Castaneda Brando with Movita Castaneda.

As a result, Marlon's day-to-day finances were perpetually tight. Several times, Marlon found final notices of non-payment of his electricity, gas, and telephone bills on the secretary's desk at the Pennebaker office.

At some point Marlon quit communicating with his father altogether. Their go-between became employee Alice Marchak, who would end up serving as Marlon's personal assistant for thirty years. She also wrote a book about life with Marlon.

So it was, when Marlon heard his father had fired an employee Marlon considered to be both a friend and a vital part of Pennebaker, there was an immediate confrontation.

"From somewhere inside me a tidal wave rose, crested and flooded, and I reduced (my father) to a heap of shambling, stuttering, fast-blinking confusion," Marlon writes with palpable relish. "I said he should consider himself fortunate to have a job, since anybody else with his qualifications would be in a poor house.

"I went over the history of our family and told him that he had ruined my mother's life and had used every opportunity to belittle me and make me feel inadequate. I took him apart with pliers, bit by bit, hunk by hunk, and distributed his psyche all over the floor. I was cold, correct and logical—no screaming or yelling—just stone frozen cold, and when he tried to make excuses, I slammed down an iron gate and reminded him what a shambles he had made of our lives. I told him that he was directly responsible for making my sisters alcoholics and that he was cold, unloving, selfish, infantile, terminally despicable and self-absorbed. I made him feel useless, helpless, hopeless and weak."

The harangue, Marlon writes, went on for "almost three hours." When Brando Sr. tried to end the confrontation, Marlon told him: "Sit down if you expect to be paid any money from this day forward.

You will listen to what your employer is telling you. I am your employer and you are something of an employee—at least you bear that name—and you will do what I tell you."

Over those three hours, Marlon continues, "I did what in thirty-three years I had never been able to, yet the whole time I was scared. I was frightened of what he would do to me. I had always been over-whelmed and intimidated by him, but the more I talked, the more strength and conviction I gained of my rightness and justification. It was like Joe Louis with Max Schmeling in their second fight: I hit him everyplace. He was naked and I was all over him like a cheap suit."

When he was done, Marlon told the old man he was fired from Pennebaker.

"Afterward," Marlon writes, "I called everybody in the family and told them what I had done, and they congratulated me. 'Well, it's about time,' my sisters said. But inside I felt tremendous after-shocks from what I had done. I thought the sky was going to fall on me because of what I had said."

A few days later, Marlon received a call from a psychiatrist. The doctor said Brando Sr. was seeing him as a patient. He wanted to enlist Marlon's cooperation because, he said, his father was "in a serious depression and on the edge of a precipice."

"Well, Doctor," Marlon quotes himself as saying. "When my father has gone over the edge of that depression and smashed himself on the rocks below—when he's hit bottom—please call me and I'll see if I can arrange something."

From then on, Marlon writes, "I always kept my father on a tight leash so that he could never come near me and never get too far away. I had him under control and never let him go."

***

I'm hacking through the jungle on the far side of motu Onetahi, the capital islet, as it were, of Teti'aroa.

In lieu of a machete, I'm beating back the brush with a strong length of driftwood. It's sharp at one end like a sword. I figure if I run into feral pigs or other unexpected trouble, I'll be able to use it to defend myself.

I have a backpack stocked with water, snacks, and the tools of my trade—two microcassette recorders, extra tapes, a 4 x 8 note pad, two pens. I'm slathered in bug spray and wrapped tight, head on a swivel, walking on the balls of my feet, stepping carefully, trying not to make too much noise. He's close, real close. I can feel him sucking me in even as I feel him repelling me.

The jungle is all weirdness and sounds—a thick, primitive, evil-feeling place, everything lewdly fertile and engorged. Plants with eight-foot leaves, vines the thickness of arms, roots like legs. Birds and insects chirp and sing, a disharmonic symphony of percussive sound with the volume jacked. A pungent blend of mold, pollen and plant rot makes my nose run. Sweat streams down my face. I spot a thick snake coiled on a limb of a tree and move past quickly, keeping my eyes glued to the serpent, like an armed robber easing his way out of a backroom poker game. Then something nearby hits the ground with a *thud*; my heart does a flip-flop. I drop to one knee, sweep the perimeter with my eyes. *What the fuck was that?*

I check the area in the direction of the sound, find a grove of coconut palms, the ground littered with fallen nuts in various states of decay. For a brief moment, in the dappled sunlight, the brown, hairy oblong spheres look like so many severed heads.

I was too young for Vietnam, but this is what it must have been like—chaotic, flarelit, and surreal, like the movie *Apocalypse Now*—a mission through the steaming jungle, a quarry I cannot see, a reason that has become too confused to unravel or understand. Like war, like love, the desire within me is strong; it burns like the midday sun. There are no odds anymore. I'm on point, I'm close, I'm walking a path that leads through the days and weeks of my mission like a main circuit cable plugged straight into Marlon. I want him. I need him. It is my mission to locate him and I will.

This is my vow to myself: If he is here, I will find him.

And if he's not here . . . I will find out where he is and go there. . . as soon as my two weeks on Teti'aroa are done. I mean, no sense wasting a good trip, right? I already pre-paid. Plus I'll need time to figure out my next steps.

In any case, failure is not an option. The rest of my life, my career, everything I've worked for . . . is balanced on the fulcrum of Marlon.

I have no watch, but I estimate I've been moving through the jungle for two hours. I have no phone, either. No GPS, not even a map. Never a Boy Scout-type, it didn't occur to me to bring along a compass. (Well, the cool survival knife I was eyeballing at REI had a compass built into the butt of the handle, and it did occur to me then as a selling point.) Anyway, a compass would have been of no use; I don't know where I'm going. Nowhere could I find a specific terrain map of motu Onetahi or any of the other islets; at this point, directions are meaningless. I have nothing to go on but instinct, a lousy sense of direction, and blind desire.

I'd started this little mission-within-a-mission at a place behind the last guest bungalow, where I followed a path into the jungle that led to the beach-front community of simple huts where Marlon's people live.

Continuing on, I found the airstrip, heat waves eddying off the asphalt, creating the kind of liquid-y mirage you see in movies. As I crossed, the bottoms of my rubber flip flops adhered slightly, each step accompanied by a slight ripping sound as the shoe detached itself from the melting tarmac. On the other side, a set of tracks led into the breathless jungle. The first day we'd arrived, as we were being led away from the plane, I'd seen Cheyenne, Marlon's daughter by Tarita, coming out of this clearing full tilt, driving a tall green farm-variety tractor, dressed in cut offs and a simple bikini top, her tawny hair streaming behind her—Lady Godiva meets the Soviet farmworker ideal, as rendered by Paul Gaugin.

Right away I knew who she was. She looked *exactly* like Marlon. It was uncanny. Marlon as a young woman, her skin kissed golden brown by the South Pacific sun.

The clearing out of which she'd appeared that day revealed a path, which led unromantically to a mound of garbage, partially buried in dirt. Just beyond was a deep empty pit, a shovel abandoned at the bottom.

Further on, I came across the remains of a cement foundation for what appeared to have been designed to be a house. Most of the clearing was reclaimed now by the ever-advancing jungle, as was a wheelbarrow, a pile of rotting lumber, and various other tools.

Next I spotted an electrical wire attached to a tree; it led another mile deeper into the bush, tree to tree, until it stopped and ran down to a transformer in the middle of a clearing. The earth was soft, but it didn't seem like anything was buried underneath. I made a mental note to return later with the shovel from the pit. *Underground complex?*

At another clearing was a large, prefab building; it appeared to be World War II-era surplus. Inside was another generator, some old bicycles, an old off-road motorcycle, and a backhoe. At the rear of the work area was a set of double doors. I grabbed an old screwdriver off the workbench and jimmied the lock. The metal was corroded and gave way easily.

Inside was a barracks or bunkhouse—a couple of small bedrooms, a bathroom, a kitchen, a bookshelf. The volumes seemed to have been carefully curated: *The Encyclopedia Americana. How to Be Rich*, by J. Paul Getty. *A Sioux Chronicle*, by George E. Hyde. *Tao, The Three Treasures*, by Bhagwan Shree Rajneesh. *Ham Antenna Construction Projects.*

Technical manuals covered everything from hydroponics to solar energy, refrigeration to birds. The audio cassettes included: "Stress Management Training Program," "Biofeedback Relaxation Training."

What books would you take with you to a deserted island?

Here was Marlon's answer.

Before setting out, I'd read an article in which Marlon talked about his early days on Teti'aroa. When he first lived here, he said, he had all kinds of forward-thinking plans for his island. He told people he wanted to bring new-age technology to Tahiti, to find ways to help modern humans live in harmony with the environment.

Later, in his autobiography, Marlon called the atoll, "a laboratory where I could experiment with solar power, aquaculture and innovative construction methods. I built one of the first sawmills in Polynesia that could turn coconut trees into lumber and felt a great sense of accomplishment. I savor the smallest details on the island.

Once I filled a hundred-foot-long piece of galvanized pipe with water, left it in the sun and produced steam through solar heating, which was very satisfying. Even the least achievement on Teti'aroa delights me."

In *Songs*, Marlon writes wistfully of his days on the atoll. He says he "spent much of the time under the thatch roof of my hut with my feet sticking out the door, looking through the shell curtains at the vivid colors of the lagoon; like the sunsets on Teti'aroa, they change constantly, depending on the sun and clouds. I sat like that for hours at a time contemplating my life, assessing my values, examining every little bird of thought that flitted through my mind.

"My life on Teti'aroa is very simple—walking, swimming, fishing, playing with the children, laughing, talking. I feel a tremendous sense of freedom there. At night there isn't much to do except look at the stars, which I love to do, and most days I don't wake up until about eleven, when I hear the fluttering of wings over my hut and birds plummet out of the sky, hit the lagoon in a quick splash and with the grace of ballerinas grab a fish for breakfast. There is fresh fruit off the trees for my breakfast, then a walk on the beach. Or I may spend an hour or two with my ham radio, talking to strangers around the world, telling them that my name is Jim Ferguson—the name of my childhood playmate—and that I live alone in Tahiti. Nobody knows I'm a movie star, and I can be like anyone else."

Marlon goes on to admit that Tet'iaroa was also a money pit. "Over the years I have spent millions on it, though it has never been profitable. Some of the money was lost because of hurricanes, some to wishful thinking and unfulfilled dreams, some to projects started and never finished, some to thieves. A lot of people robbed me—a few who worked for me, others who were con men and came to the island promising to do things they never did—took my money and then disappeared. One operator promised to produce lobsters in the lagoon through aquaculture, and I invited about twenty scientists to the island with their wives. There was a lot of wonderful talk about harvesting lobsters that came to nothing. Storms frequently struck the island; every time we finished a new building, it seemed that another hurricane came along and damaged it. But I enjoyed all of it."

It comes as no surprise that during the period he spent the most time in Tahiti, Marlon made one clunker after another: *The Ugly American* (1963), *Bedtime Story* (1964), *Morituri* (1965), *The Chase* (1966), *The Appaloosa* (1966), *A Countess from Hong Kong* (1967), *The Night of the Following Day* (1969), *Candy* (1968).

"I need money, I make a film," he said during that period. It was obvious.

Now, hacking through the jungle, two hours into my search, I'm following another trail. I come upon the ruins of what appears to be a *marae*, a Polynesian place of worship—an outdoor temple for offerings, dances, and rituals. All that remains are old stones arranged in a rectangle, the dimensions approximately ten feet long and three feet wide. I wonder: Is it a foundation for a building that once stood? The base of a raised platform? I make a mental note to do more research.

In antiquity, Teti'aroa was owned by a Tahitian royal family, the Pomares. The island served as a summer residence for chiefs and *Aroioi*, members of a South Seas religious sect that venerated the war god 'Oro. On Teti'aroa, nobles entertained themselves with song, dance, fishing, feasting, and religious festivals. It was also a special place for the *Ariori* to practice their custom of *ha'apori'a*, which included gorging oneself to gain weight and staying out of the sun to lighten the skin—fat and pale was, at the time, an outward sign of prosperity. Party members would arrive by sailing canoe, repair to shady groves, eat fish and coconut, and have their way with young girls who were brought here for those purposes. Some say virgins were sacrificed in *maraes* like this one; some say the sacrifices were made of people who broke taboos. Some say there was cannibalism; some say the cannibalism was limited to the eating of an enemy's eye.

At any rate, there is an eerie feeling about the place, a palpable force, a vibration. I can only imagine what may have happened here. I push on.

At last the jungle breaks on the far side of the island. There is a broad sandy beach; the blue water of the lagoon laps peacefully at the shoreline. The sun is high overhead, so I'm not sure exactly which direction I'm facing. I figure I've been out for three or four hours. My skin burns, my entire body throbs with cuts and welts; the bug spray seems to have had little effect in this primordial setting.

I refresh myself in the ocean, a quick little dip, and then I continue to walk along the shoreline, seeking relief from the heat. A little farther, I find a peaceful inlet.

And a house.

Upon closer inspection, the house is really a series of houses, a network of vaguely Japanese-style pavilions, constructed mostly of coconut wood, with a crude boardwalk connecting and unifying the separate structures into a large rectangular compound. The walls are made of large sheets of Plexiglas, framed with wood. An arrangement of ropes and pulleys leads me to speculate that the Plexi is meant to be raised when inhabited. A cool breeze blows through the ironwood trees planted all around; the fine long needles whisper and sway.

At the moment, everything is nailed shut, giving the place the feeling of an exhibit at a museum. One pavilion has a stove and a sink, another has a long, low, Japanese-style table for dining, another appears to be a pantry, with rows of empty shelves. There are seven pavilions in all, stretching perhaps 200 feet on the long side of the rectangle.

The last bungalow is the largest. Inside is a simple bed made of coconut wood, the same style as in my guest bungalow, overhung with the same mosquito netting. There is also a roughhewn chair and desk.

The frames around the windows in this last pavilion are not only nailed like the others. They are also screwed, padlocked, and secured with two-by-fours. Clearly someone doesn't want anyone gaining entrance. It is by far the most security I have seen on Marlon's island. There is personal stuff all over the place.

A can of bug spray, a jar of Nescafé instant coffee, a wooden salad bowl, a refrigerator, toothpicks in a shot glass. Tools piled on the floor, a bird cage covered with a towel, a driftwood sculpture, an African fright mask, several strings of worry beads, the bleached skull of an animal. A pair of fly swatters hang from the beam that supports the roof. Near the bed is a beat-up set of conga drums.

Wait a minute.

Conga drums?

Marlon played the congas!

Immediately I remember a bit I'd read about Marlon partying at a club in Harlem with James Baldwin, and how he paid a conga drummer five bucks to sit in with the band. Later, in 1955, Marlon gave a live, microwave-link-televised tour of his Hollywood Hills home to the famous newsman Edward R. Murrow. Arriving at a room that housed his collection of drums, Marlon gave Murrow a mini lecture on the history of the conga drum, followed by an "impromptu" performance. Later in life, Marlon patented a tuning system for conga drums, which he developed with the help of Latin jazz percussionist Poncho Sanchez.

This has *got* to be Marlon's room.

Holy shit!

I have found Marlon's *stuff*!

I pull my reporter's pad out of my backpack and begin taking notes—marble desktop, flowered blue tablecloth, nail adorned with shell necklaces—hoovering every detail like a line of drug, buzzed beyond belief. I have come so far. Now I am here, separated from Marlon Brando's possessions by only a half inch thickness of Plexiglas. Things he has touched. Things he has used. Things he cares about. Imagine what useful information could be inside those two small metal file cabinets! What could be waiting to be discovered inside the drawers of the desk!

Petal brand facial tissue (white), forks (three), a coffee cup, magazines: *Popular Science, Scientific American, Time, Newsweek, Sports Illustrated.*

And then . . . something else registers.

The magazines have mailing labels!

The subscriber's name and address are affixed to every one of the front covers, as with all magazine subscriptions.

Marlon Brando
XXXX Mulholland Drive,
Beverly Hills, CA.

It's Marlon Brando's address in Beverly Hills!

I am overcome with joy, with adrenaline, with purpose.

I jump off the porch, race back through the jungle.

His address, his address. I've got his address!

And now I want more.

I run for thirty or forty minutes, jumping over logs and smashing through vines and bushes like a steeplechase runner, taking what I think will be a straighter line this time, heading toward the big, World War II-era structure I found earlier.

Once there, I search the floor, the shelves, the peg board, the walk-in closet.

Finally, in one corner of the room, I find what I'm looking for.

Rusty, three feet long.

A crowbar.

I pick it up, weigh the heft of it in my hand.

Who knows what's inside the drawers?

All at once I am overcome by an intense wave of nausea. I feel dizzy. Sweat pops out on the top of my head, flows into my eyes. My heart is beating so fast and hard it feels like it's trying to kick its way free from the prison of my ribcage.

What the fuck am I doing?

I fall to my knees. The crowbar falls from my hand, clangs on the cement floor.

And then it hits me:

Marlon Brando is not on this island.

From what I could observe through the Plexiglass, the *newest* magazines in his room are more than a year old. His place is shut tight. There is nowhere else on this island for him to be. It's the largest of the 13. I've looked everywhere. I've searched in grids. I've been all over the place.

On the way in, the plane had buzzed low over the entire atoll before landing. We were no more than 100 feet above each of the islets. One thing is sure: If there was anything to see on any other motu—a clearing, a structure, an irregular shape in the unrelenting tangle of the thick green jungle—surely there would have been some sign.

Maybe Simone is telling the truth.

Maybe Marlon is not here.

Come to think of it, on our first walk, Teri'i had told Angelina that his buddy, Marlon's son, Teihotu, is in California for Christmas. She'd even translated that part. Supposedly, he went there to help Marlon.

That's where they are. I am sure of it.

At Marlon's house, on the tippy top of the Mullholland Mountains.

And now I have the address.

***

An hour later, I return to my bungalow. There's a handwritten note on the door, wedged between the palm fronds.

> Mr. Sager (Mike):
> I have taken the 15:00 plane back to Papeete.
> Good luck finding Marlon!
> Angelina
>
> P.S. Please give my salary to Benji.

***

Teri'i's hut is on the beach, no more than thirty feet from the lagoon, plywood and thatch with a millionaire's view.

He's got 95-Rock from Papeete playing on a boom box—after all, we are only 50 miles from the bustling mainland. The DJ sounds the same as every rock radio jock in America, except he's speaking what I gather is a creole of French and Tahitian.

Apparently, Teri'i has just harvested his grow. There's abundant weed—wet, green, and skunky. The high doesn't last very long, but it works fine if you roll huge joints and keep puffing, like a cigar, only *with* inhaling. Teri'i's rolling style resembles the European custom, cone shaped and employing a bit of folded matchbook cover as a filter or crutch (as opposed to the more primitive, burrito-shaped joints more popular at the time in America). As he seems to be with every task he undertakes, Teri'i is exceedingly skilled in cone-rolling. The longer I know him the more I come to see him as a kind of perfect man—utterly devoid of care, completely adapted, totally at one with his place in the universe.

We sit on two wooden vegetable crates outside the door of his little bungalow. During the heat of the day, a small grove of coconut palms provides a delightful patch of shade. We don't have much language in common, but we seem to enjoy each other's company. Marijuana has always worked for me as a universal language, an ice breaker. Like sharing a beer, except a little more edgy, and never ugly like drink. Essentially, we were breaking the law together, an instant bond.

"Have you ever seen Marlon's movies?" I ask. As yet I haven't told anyone what I'm actually doing here, but asking about Marlon seems pretty natural, being that we're on his atoll. I'm sure I'm not the first. I name a few of his movies: "*Apocalypse Now, Superman, Godfather—*"

"*Le Pe're!*"

"French for *The Godfather?*"

"Oui, oui. *Le Pe're.*"

"Is good for you, this movie?"

"Is okay. I no like movie," Teri'i says, exaggerating his frown—an ongoing game of charades increases our shared vocabulary by some small measure. "Is too much bad. No good for eyes. I like look sunset."

"Sunset *is* beautiful here, yes?"

"Yes. Sunset. And sky. And sea. All day color change. Is not only one sea, is many seas."

He pauses a moment to gather his words. "Here is very good for me," he says, pressing his fist to his heart, then sweeping outward his open hand.

In the days that follow, I come often to Teri'i's bungalow. With my next move—a trip to Los Angeles—on hold for the duration of my pre-paid stay, I'm officially on vacation.

I show up to Teri'i's place in the late afternoons with a plastic bag of beers from the voluntary bar. I'm not sure exactly what part Teri'i plays in the hotel enterprise. There are only a few bungalows in use. None of the employees seem to work very hard, or even at all, mostly. Someone cleans your room every few days. You can never predict what time they'll show up or who it will be. Maybe Teri'i's main job is to be Teihotu's friend?

And since Teihotu isn't here, it seems his main responsibility is simply *being*.

Here on this beautiful atoll, he has everything he needs. He is living his life in the present, walking around barefoot, his private parts concealed comfortably beneath a length of hand-painted rectangular cloth, expertly wrapped around his waist. His state of grace is shared, seemingly, by all of the two or three dozen inhabitants of the island—sheltered within Marlon's warm embrace.

Inexplicably, Teri'i seems to like me. He keeps inviting me back. When we run out of words, we sit on our respective crates for long periods, each of us tilted back precariously against one of the coco wood support beams. We stare out silently toward the lagoon, the horizon. I never once speak of Angelina, and neither does he. It doesn't seem important. It's as if she was never here, a footprint the ocean has washed away.

But still, it nags at me:

Why did she leave? What happened?

Did it have something to do with Teri'i? With one of the others?

Maybe she thought I was asking her to do something unethical. Did she feel as though I was asking her to rat out her own people?

Or was she just creeped out by the whole crazy vibe?

Find Marlon Brando. *Are you kidding me?*

Of course, some questions, large and small, can never be answered. And anyway, I have no time to dwell. It's not for trivial reasons of the heart or loins that I'm spending two weeks, at the expense of the *Washington Post*, on Marlon Brando's private atoll. It's a job, after all. Angelina was hired to help facilitate the job. Odd though her performance may have been, she was actually successful in helping me to break the ice. My friendship with Teri'i is the tangible result.

In the way of small groups, Teri'i's acceptance of me has led to friendships with the others as well. Maybe they really like me. Maybe they feel sorry for me because my "date" ditched me and left the island. Or maybe they know something I don't know about Angelina? Either way, it doesn't matter. At least Angelina didn't expose me as an undercover journalist as I had feared.

For the duration of my visit, I hang out whenever possible with Teri'i and the other men—with Charles, Popi and Serge, primarily. I try to do as they do: bury my feet in the warm sand up to my ankles, stare out beyond the coral reef at the limitless and ever-morphing ocean.

As the days pass, I feel more and more at peace. I notice my motor slowing, slowing, shutting down. The space inside my body becomes quiet. The obsessive inner monologue, the Talmudic-level of perseveration, the constant critical voice that narrates, debates, dissects, reads- in, examines, and re-examines everything everything *everything* . . .

All of that sputters and slows.

I stop thinking about my ambitions, my career, my art, my headlong rush to achieve whatever the fuck it is I'm trying so hard to achieve.

I even stop thinking about my hunt for Marlon Brando.

Instead, I try to concentrate on simply *being.*

And then I concentrate on trying to not try.

I play barefoot soccer on the beach with the other guys (there is not much inter-sex mixing during the day) and loll in the salty, buoyant, lukewarm lagoon with them afterward, floating like hippos, with our noses just above the waterline, our weightless arms like outriggers, toes grazing the soft sand on the bottom. I learn how to spot a fish by the ripple it makes in the water, how to navigate an outrigger canoe through the shallows of the lagoon using the different hues as a depth chart.

Because I am a man of olive color, my skin tans deeply. With my hoop earring, beard, and shaved head—an unusual choice for the era, I might add, a full three years before basketball legend Michael Jordan popularized the look by shaving his own head in 1989—I am taken, by some of the new guests, for an employee of Marlon's hotel.

They approach tentatively, as tourists do. "Where's the good fishing?" they ask.

I tell them what Teri'i told me: "Good fish everywhere. Just throw in line."

At night, when the generator is off and the guests are asleep, there are a million stars. After Dirty Old Bob's closes, Marlon's people move as a group toward their own little community. There are a couple more picnic tables here. A small fire burns in the pit used sometimes for cooking pigs. There are guitars and a set of congas. Everybody sings. Matahi teaches me the chords and I grab a guitar and play along. We drink and smoke and we sing some more. I feel part of something warm, something old, something very right.

I find myself saying, "Here is very good." I press my fist to my heart, sweep my open hand outward.

Finally, *finally*, I meet Tarita, the mistress of the atoll. Marlon's love interest in *Mutiny on the Bounty* is the mother of two of his children—Tehotu and Cheyenne—and the co-guardian of two more girls, close relatives of Tarita's whom she and Marlon adopted.

I recognize Tarita instantly. She looks as if she's hasn't aged a day since the movie. I'm not embarrassed to admit that back at home, late at night, when I was doing my movie research—transcribing Marlon's dialog and taking other notes—I rewound *Bounty* a time or two (or three?). Especially the scene where Tarita dances seductively for Fletcher Christian, the handsome young sea captain played by Marlon.

Tarita is 45 now, still beautiful and lithe. Her warm smile strikes me dumb as she takes my hand to shake. Hers is warm, strong, sinewy, and calloused. For one brief moment I want to kneel or kiss her hand or something equally dramatic.

Luckily, I do not.

Tarita was a waitress when she was picked from a group of sixteen girls to audition for the part of Maimiti, the daughter of a Tahitian chief who is given as a wife to Mr. Christian.

After arriving in Tahiti to choose his leading lady, as he'd been promised, Marlon set up shop in a hotel in Papeete. He brought each of the sixteen prescreened candidates into his second-story room. After greeting them and offering a beverage, he threatened to jump out the window.

Tarita got the part, he would later recall, because she was the one who giggled least.

"He attracted me and at the same time he scared me," Tarita would later write in a memoir, published in French and German, *Marlon, My Love and My Torment.*

Born in Bora Bora to a fisherman, Tarita's ancestry was French Polynesian and Chinese. Her acting career began and ended with *Mutiny*; afterwards, thanks to Marlon, she was able to resume the quiet island life of her youth—if a life that included Marlon could ever be simple—supplemented by trips to houses they owned on Tahiti and on her home island.

On Teti'aroa, according Marlon's people, Tarita spends a lot of her time gardening. She fishes almost every day, usually with her mother and all three of her daughters.

In the late afternoons, from the bar stool at Dirty Bob's, I can see them fishing in the lagoon: five females from three generations in an outrigger canoe, throwing hooks baited with squid over the side, each in a slightly different direction to avoid tangled lines . . . pulling up fish after fish.

The day after our first meeting, when I see Tarita and her party begin to paddle back to shore, I walk over to give Popi a hand helping the women and girls out of the boat, then help him drag it onto the beach, above the tideline. Then I help him carry the fish—it will be tonight's "catch of the day"—to the kitchen.

During the process, Tarita and I exchange smiles, then I avert my eyes. No words pass between us. I have no idea what she thinks of me. Maybe she's wondering why the hell this guest is helping the help. Maybe she takes the respect for granted. Or maybe she's heard about Angelina and figures I'm keeping myself busy to deal with the grief of our breakup.

The next day, I again play Johnny-on-the-Spot. As I'm reaching down into the canoe to grab one of the strings of fish, Tarita steps toward me.

"Thank you," she says. "You different like other guest."

For a long moment I am paralyzed, stuck in the sand as if in concrete, holding the string of fish, my elbow at 90 degrees in the manner someone in mid-performance of a bicep curl—I'm sorry, my knowledge of fish taxonomy is limited to the labels inside my local fish monger's glass case, so I can't tell you what kind of fish I was holding, but I can say there were three of them on the line, and they weighed about as much as a 20-pound dumbbell.

"It is nothing," I say. My heart does a little dance.

Cheyenne smiles at me, too. Her youth and beauty are such I feel compelled to look away. Who could have predicted what the next decade would bring for this benighted young woman?

***

My last night on Marlon's island, Tarita invites me to dinner at her large bungalow.

I am one of ten at a family-style meal. I have no idea if this is a special treat or if all guests are afforded this pleasure, which feels a little bit like a Polynesian island version of dining at the captain's table.

At this point, other than Angelina's little off-script outburst at the very top of my visit, when she blabbed everything to Simone, I'm pretty sure nobody on Marlon's island knows I'm a journalist.

As far as I observed, during the entirety of my two weeks stay, I have not, on any occasion at all, comported myself in any manner that might be construed as behavior common to journalists on the job. Not once have I acted nosey or forward or pushy or demanding or entitled. Not once have I gone out of my lane as a proper and well-behaved guest; I have been nothing but the *mensch* I was raised by my parents to be, a man who knows what is right and acts accordingly.

(Okay, I ran back through the jungle willy-nilly to the shed for the crowbar, and I picked it up. But I never used it, I ended up putting it back exactly where I found it. As far as the broken lock, well, you can ding me a few karma points, but I don't know if that's necessarily something a journalist would regularly do. Probably it would be construed as more an act of vandalism, or illegal trespass, or perhaps breaking and entering. Something criminal. We are only humans, after all. We have our lower instincts. We are sometimes misguided. Maybe this is why all the great religions offer systems of penance and forgiveness.)

Anyway, even if I wanted to act like a journalist and ask rude, direct questions to any of the people at Tarita's dinner table—or instead probe subtly for detail using the device of pleasant-but-guided conversation—it would be impossible because, from what I can tell, nobody at dinner speaks much English. I don't even know exactly what I'm eating—but all of it is fresh and simple and delicious. In between sips and chews, I smile beatifically. I try my best to simply *be*: to absorb and imprint upon myself the prevailing atmosphere of peace and tranquility.

Later that night, stretched out for the last time beneath my mosquito netting in my coconut wood bed, the moonlight streams brightly through the window, illuminating the lazy circles of smoke drifting upwards from the green mosquito coils set around the room. The jungle is loud with nocturnal energy. I feel pure and happy and relaxed and unencumbered.

My mind drifts forward to the time I will meet Marlon. Surely, once brought together, the two of us will get along famously. If his atoll is any reflection of the man, I know I'll like him.

And perhaps, because I appreciate it so much here, and because my sojourn has earned me a glimpse into his soul, maybe it's not too much to speculate that Marlon will like me, too?

We could collaborate on his autobiography. He's never done a proper book from his own point of view. I can be his voice. I know that now. Perhaps we can come down here together to Teti'aroa, and he'll set me up on my *own* island. There's one right across the lagoon that seems to be totally empty. I could paddle over every morning to interview him for the book, and then paddle back afterwards. To write. To live. To simply be. This is very good.

I haven't found Marlon—not exactly, not yet. But I do feel that being here on his island, I have found something of the man himself, an important something, a beginning of an understanding of this complex and enlightened being, a man who would do all this: buy a paradisiacal atoll in the middle of the ocean, found a small peaceful kingdom, people it with gentle natives, shelter them with goodness.

A man whose wisdom could surely help to solve some of the grave and pressing problems faced by our world.

As the dawn breaks, I'm still awake, buzzing with good health and excitement and plans.

I can't wait to meet him.

***

My new friends accompany me to the airstrip.

We form a little procession; the scuffle of our flip-flops on the sandy path stirs small clouds of dust as we saunter along. Teri'i carries my duffle bag on his head, making a game of balancing it with no hands. What a specimen. If this is what paradise was like, maybe Adam was similarly ripped? And even though I demurred repeatedly, Popi has my backpack over one shoulder. On the tarmac, Matahi plays his guitar and sings a sad but sweet Polynesian song and everyone claps. Simone floats a floral lei over my head and kisses both my cheeks.

I know for certain I'll be back—possibly in the company of Marlon.

***

Two hours later, I'm back at the Hotel Ibis.

I settle up with Benji on behalf of Angelina. He smiles and acts hotel-employee-fake, exactly as he did before, his blue back hair gleaming, furrowed with long tidy rows, carefully plowed by the teeth of his comb from the crown of his pompadour to his duck tail.

Aside from exchanging an envelope of American dollars, neither of us brings up Angelina.

A series of events to be filed forever under WTF.

But as it turned out, she did what I needed her to do, a service to the mission, well worth the *Post's* money.

The next morning, at breakfast on the terrace, I am staring out into the busy harbor, toward the horizon, missing Teti'aroa, when I remember something Teri'i had told me. Something about Marlon having an office in Papeete run by a woman named Cynthia. Our lack of a common language precluded any greater detail. But it's a lead. I am pretty sure at this point I know Marlon's exact location—he is hunkered down in his compound on Mulholland with his son Teihotu. But I know damn well the address alone isn't going to do me any good. I'm not going to be able to walk up to the door and just knock. Teri'i had also mentioned something about fierce German shepherd dogs guarding the place. I'd come a long way, but my mission was far from over. I still needed an in.

I call the travel agency. As a new and possibly future client, I wonder: Could they please assist me in finding some kind of corporate representative for the Hotel Teti'aroa here in Papeete?

***

Cynthia is found in the Bureau de Teti'aroa, a small office located in a minimalist, third-world-style corporate building at Faa'a Airport. Later I will learn she's a former airline attendant, originally from Maui, Hawaii; she runs all of Marlon's Tahitian interests. With my Hawaiian shirt and flip-flops—and my introduction from the travel agency's owner—I guess she figures me for an enthusiastic tourist with a few more questions about the hotel. Or possibly a businessman with a proposition?

"What can we do for you, Mr. Sager?" she asks, pleasantly enough, standing and walking around one side of her desk to greet me. "I hope there were no *problems* with your stay at the hotel."

"No no no! Or course not! It was amazing," I say, altogether truthfully. Like a dean giving out a diploma, I move to shake her offered hand with my right, meanwhile proffering a business card with my left. (Though I left the *Post* nearly three years ago, I figure it's okay to use a leftover card, no?)

In the moment it takes her to process the information embossed there upon the small, white, rectangular piece of card stock—surely the logo is instantly recognizable—I settle myself in a seat in the visitor's chair across from her . . .

. . . which triggers a full, movie-style flashback: The last time I was in this position, chair in front of desk, I was pitching to Jay Lovinger.

Go to Tahiti and find Marlon Brando.

Cynthia looks down at me, her eyes wide with disbelief. "You're a journalist?"

The tone in her voice—such grave disappointment. And Fear. And revulsion. She might have just said, "You're a child molester?"

"I raise my hands to her in low surrender. "Please. I'm *not* here for an interview—"

"Good, because I can't answer *any* questions," she says with utter disdain.

"I promise I'll do all the talking," I say. "Could you spare *five minutes* to hear me out?"

She takes a seat behind the protective bastion of her desk and crosses her arms. Her eyelids lower almost imperceptibly. She's too polite to throw me out.

Over the next few minutes, in distinctly measured tones, I deliver what might be the most impassioned speech in a life of impassioned speeches—all the way back to my days as a counselor at Camp Timber Ridge, when I was a perennial choice for Color War captain. A five-five guy learns to use his mouth.

"I am not looking for a scoop, not in the conventional sense," I begin. "And I don't give a damn about actors or movies. I'm here on a much more important mission."

I brief Cynthia on my assignment, my preparation, my obsession (well, I tread a little lightly on that part). I tell her about watching all of Marlon's movies, *every single one of them several times*, and transcribing all the dialog. I tell her about going to the United States Library of Congress, the nation's hallowed repository of recorded knowledge, and reading everything I could find.

I tell her about hiring Angelina, going to Teti'aroa. About hanging with Marlon's people. About finding Marlon's compound on the other side of the island and feeling how *he* must have felt.

And, I tell her about my connection with Tarita, how I helped with her boat, her fish, her gardening, and how I was invited to dine in her bungalow with her family and friends. I quote her saying so adorably, "You different like other guest."

"Visiting to Marlon's island, reading about him, learning about his life—I have come to think of Marlon as a visionary," I continue. "A *visionary*, Cynthia. He was one of the first actors to produce and direct. He was one of the first to get percentage of gross. He was one of the first to study Eastern religions. He went to Southeast Asia before anybody even knew about the war in Vietnam. He gave up a starring role in *Butch Cassidy and the Sundance Kid* because he was too grief-stricken over the death of Martin Luther King Jr. Did you know that, Cynthia?

"Marlon bought an island and turned it into his own little utopian paradise. I've seen his little civilization. I've seen his collection of books and magazines. I've even sat under what I'm sure must be his favorite tree—and it became my favorite tree. Never in my life have I felt anything like the peace I felt swinging in the hammock outside Marlon's bungalow.

"Let me put it this way, Cynthia," I continue, moving toward my point. "America *needs* Marlon. I know Marlon has ideas. He has foresight. He's way ahead of the curve. I think he can help make the world a better place to live.

"I've been sent by one of the great newspapers of the world, all expenses paid, just to seek his advice. Think of that. The *Washington Post*—the newspaper powerful enough to unseat a crooked American president and to keep democracy free—that very newspaper has sent me to seek advice from Marlon Brando.

"The world is shit, Cynthia. You have to agree. We need to ask him: *What comes next?*"

As Cynthia listens to my sermon, her pupils grow wide. She's leaning forward, her elbows on the desk, and she's nodding her head, nodding, nodding, I can plainly see she is in total agreement with what I'm saying, she is with me *one hundred percent*, nodding her head, nodding her head, a member of the choir. She's been with him fifteen years. Of course she thinks Marlon is brilliant and important.

The funny thing is this: I'm starting to believe it, too.

"Cynthia, I know Marlon is in Los Angeles. In fact, I know you were just there, staying at his compound. You know how I know this, Cynthia? It's because after two weeks on Teti'aroa, spending time with Marlon's people, they learned to trust me. They hung around with me every day. They perceived me as a decent human being. Even Tarita invited me to dinner in her bungalow. In her bungalow, Cynthia, with all three girls and Granmere!

"Please, can you help? I need to see Marlon. It can be off the record for the first meeting. He can inspect me up and down. I'll follow whatever conditions he needs. All I'm asking is for him to hear me out.

"I'm flying to Los Angeles tomorrow. Can you get me some time with him? As much as he's willing to give the *Washington Post*. Five minutes. Five hours. Five days. I'll listen for as long as he wants to talk. *Any subject! Nothing is off the table.* And I'll print *exactly* what he wants me to print. Please, tell him that, Cynthia. *Please.* Tell him I'll print his words without any editing—"

Just then the phone rings.

Cynthia picks up the receiver. She seems happy to have been interrupted; she lunges for the phone somewhat in the manner of a passenger fallen overboard lunging for a lifebuoy.

She speaks French into the receiver. The conversation goes back and forth. She has her face turned, so I see her profile. She appears to be looking out the window at the modest airport control tower in the middle distance.

At some point, Cynthia holds my card out in front of her and says my name, and then she says "the *Washington Post*," and then she listens some more. As she does, she eyeballs me appraisingly. I can't tell what she's thinking.

Suddenly, her face brightens. Some kind of line has been crossed.

She rings off, replaces the phone in the cradle. She turns her chair back 90 degrees so she's facing forward again.

"That was Tarita," she says. She lets the name steep in the humid air between us for a few moments, as if she's deciding what to say.

"I told her you were here," she says. "She said you were a nice person."

"She was *so cool*," I say, feeling pretty good. "So down to earth. And so beautiful."

"She was surprised to hear you were a journalist."

"Yeah? What else did she say?"

"She said I should call Marlon and tell him you're coming to L.A. When are you leaving?"

***

In July, 1965, Marlon was visiting the Navajo Reservation in Arizona, where he was received as a hero for his efforts toward justice for Native Americans. There he met an old medicine woman. He asked if she could "tell anything about me just by looking."

The woman dipped her hand into a box beside her and sprinkled yellow cornflowers over Marlon's head and shoulders, letting them fall around him like colorful snow.

"She said alcohol had played a very important part in my life," Marlon writes, "and that I was about to be struck by lightning. As she said it, I felt a strange sensation streak through my nervous system."

Then the medicine woman told him, "Both your parents are dead."

Marlon corrected her. "One of them is dead—my mother. But not my father."

The woman said no more.

After he left the woman's dwelling, Marlon writes, "within minutes, I was informed that there was a telephone call for me at the tribal office."

It was his sister, Jocelyn, calling. Brando Sr. had just died.

"We both laughed, and I joked, 'And not a moment too soon!'" Marlon writes. I imagine him saying it in the voice of Groucho Marx, working his eyebrows; from an early age he'd been a talented mimic.

That night, as Marlon began to drift off to sleep, he writes, "I had a vision of my father walking down a sidewalk away from me, then turning around to look at me, a slump-shouldered Willy Loman with a faint smile on his face. When he got to the edge of eternity, he stopped and looked back again. With his eyes downcast, he said: 'I did the best I could, kid.'

"Then he turned away again. I knew he was looking for my mother."

***

About six years after his father died, Marlon found himself on the set of the controversial movie *Last Tango in Paris*, an erotic drama directed by Bernardo Bertolucci.

In the film, Marlon portrays a middle-aged American who meets a young Parisian woman at an apartment showing. The man has been recently widowed. The woman is soon to be married. The two enter into a deep, erotic, and wrenching affair—without ever revealing their names or identities to one another.

The film's depictions of sexual violence led to international controversy. Upon release in the United States, the film was rated X, usually a box office killer. It became one of the top ten grossing films of the year.

As was becoming the norm, during filming, Marlon refused to memorize his lines. Instead, handwritten cue cards were posted around the set, leaving Bertolucci with the problem of keeping them out of the frame. At one point, Brando asked Bertolucci if he could write lines on Schneider's ass. He was refused.

Perhaps to avoid altogether the problem of learning lines, Bertolucci urged Marlon to improvise from his own experiences. In the movie, Marlon's character, Paul, talks of his father being a drunk and a "whore fucker." His mother, he says, was "poetic and also a drunk," who'd sometimes be gone when he came home from school, off at a bar or locked up in jail. He told the story of the time he was dressed for a date and his father forced him to milk the cow. He talked about digging ditches, and how his mother taught him to love nature. "That," Marlon's character says, "was the most she could do."

Later, the film's female star, Maria Schneider, would speak publicly of the traumas of making the movie, particularly a scene in which Marlon's character anally rapes Schneider's character using a stick of butter as a lubricant. Though the sex act was simulated, with Marlon still wearing his underclothes for the scene, the butter smearing was not. Apparently, at the time of filming, Bertolucci insisted Schneider be kept unaware of the bit with the butter, something he and Marlon had come up with together.

Though Marlon insisted he protested the part of the plan in which Schneider was kept in the dark, it was to no avail; no doubt he had run out of favors by then. Schneider later told the press she felt as violated by the director as her character had felt violated in the movie. She also said Marlon had confessed that he, too, felt violated by Bertolucci's "very manipulative" methods.

For his work on the film, Marlon won the National Society of Film Critics Award for best actor, and also the New York Film Critics Circle Award for best actor. In remarks to the press, Schneider never blamed Marlon for his role in her traumatic experience. She was quoted as saying "the best part of making the film" had been getting to know him.

While Marlon had never been a director's dream—as far back as Shattuck Academy, he'd played the beautiful bad boy, a person who could hypnotize you with his charm . . . and then then disappoint you . . . and then resent you for it. As he grew older, if it was possible, his reputation for being difficult on sets became even worse. Besides being unwilling to memorize his lines, he was uninterested in taking direction. Or he'd become unable to continue filming unless capricious demands were met. That he could still command hefty fees for his work only complicated matters.

In 1980, Marlon appeared in *The Formula*, with a cast of heavyweight co-stars, including George C. Scott and Sir Arthur John Gielgud. A mystery set in post-World War II Germany, involving former Nazis and a plot to wreck the world's oil-based economy with a secret synthetic fuel, the film was roundly panned.

When awards season came around, Marlon was nominated for a number of snarky awards, newly in fashion, including the Stinkers Bad Movie Awards (Most Annoying Fake Accent, Male) and the Razzies (Worst Supporting Actor).

Thereafter, Marlon announced his retirement from acting.

For the next decade, he would concentrate on political causes, his growing brood of children, and Teti'aroa.

***

If it can be said my hunt for Marlon Brando has so far resembled (at least in my own mind) the mission undertaken by Martin Sheen/Captain Willard in *Apocalypse Now*, my arrival at Los Angeles International Airport reminds me of the point in the movie where Captain Willard reaches the Do Lung Bridge. Singled out by cinephiles as a classic, the scene is Francis Ford Coppola's Dantesque vision of the last U.S. outpost on Captain Willard's covert journey up the river into Cambodia to find and assassinate Marlon's rogue Army officer, Col. Kurtz.

Remember the scene? Tracers and flares and weird fires burning against the black sky. Psychedelic music, tripped-out soldiers, machine gunners firing randomly into the darkness, fighting a spectral enemy. No one in charge.

After two weeks barefoot on Marlon's island, singing around the firepit and eating fresh fish straight out of the kaleidoscopic lagoon, that's how it feels when I arrive at LAX Airport.

It is cold for Los Angeles, fifty degrees, and raining. The sky is brown at the edges, a particulate haze that makes for colorful sunsets, kind of like the skies in *Apocalypse Now*, especially during fire season.

A photographer friend picks me up. His name is Jeff. We're supposed to go together to the Marshall Islands to do another story, the other part of my contract with the *Post*, about the refugees from the Bikini Atoll who'd been kicked off their land during World War II so that the U.S. could test its nuclear arsenal. (The place was made completely uninhabitable. Some of the beaches actually turned to glass.) Given the originally agreed-upon deadlines, I'm late starting because I'm not yet finished with Marlon.

Because he's a good friend, and because we do the same work with different tools, Jeff understands I have to see this mission to conclusion before I can think about starting the next.

Because I've blown through my expense account—another experience he knows well—he's arranged for me to stay with his parents, Armony and Jack, in the Sherman Oaks section of the San Fernando Valley.

Staying with Jeff's family is actually more perfect than it might sound. Armony is incredibly warm, an embracing mother to all in her orbit. And Jack is a therapist. Which makes me feel a little more in control. Sherman Oaks is just down the hill from the mountain ridge along which snakes the exclusive and picturesque Mulholland Drive—not at all far from Marlon's place.

I'd met Jeff when he was walking across the United States, from Barstow, California, to New York City to Washington, D.C., with some 800 anti-nuclear protesters and their caravan of supplies. It was my first story for the *Post* magazine, just before Jay Lovinger arrived. The rag-tag assembly of protestors, really a makeshift city on a very long hike, billed themselves as The Great Peace March for Global Nuclear Disarmament. All of the participants had put their lives on hold to make this walk across the country, a journey of 3,700 miles, nine months, and many campsites, at a time with no cellphones or Internet.

I caught up with the march in Pennsylvania. By then they were exhausted but determined, weary in spirit but buoyed by the adrenaline rush of the finish line in D.C. I walked the last 200 miles. It was pretty inspiring, especially when the Capitol dome came in to view.

It's been a while since Jeff and I have been together. When you're an outsider spending a lot of time with a huge group of true believers like the peace marchers, and you find another outsider who understands the need for a little sarcasm and gallows humor, you can get close to a person pretty fast. Like war correspondents, we were both living behind enemy lines for a time, and there we forged a friendship that would last though other missions as well.

Now, as he motors up the 405 Freeway toward his folks' house, we share the usual goofiness and personal updates. Of course, it isn't long before the conversation turns to Marlon.

I start telling Jeff about the story . . . when all of a sudden, I get this queasy feeling.

I pull my backpack up from the floor and into my lap. I rummage all the various zipper compartments a couple of times, growing more and more frantic as I realize:

I'd left my reporter's notebook in the seat back pocket on the plane.

It has everything! All my notes and sources and contact numbers.

Including the name and number of the contact in Los Angeles Cynthia had given me.

Including Marlon's address.

Who memorizes numbers when they're written down?

Do you?

We're driving in the beat-up mini pickup truck with camper shell that had also made the cross-country journey with the great peace march, carrying Jeff, his assistant, and all of his equipment. It could definitely use a new set of shocks and springs. Each bump in the road sets the car jiggling, as if the suspension is made of Jello.

Advised of the problem, Jeff hesitates not. Checking the rear view mirror briefly, he cuts the steering wheel hard right and we lurch across six lanes of traffic on one of the busiest highways in America.

I clench the hand-hold above the passenger window, brace myself with the other hand against the center console. I'm so angry, so fucking pissed, so utterly disappointed, I could literally strangle myself, if that is even possible. It's all my own fault. What a fucking idiot! Sometime during my flight to Los Angeles, during the dusky nether-hours of my seemingly endless coach class trajectory north across the Pacific, I'd fallen victim to a sudden and intense wave of uncertainty—call it anxiety, panic, fear of failure, what have you—that completely dissolved the composite material of my confindence, like the tide washing over a sandcastle.

In my panic, all I could think about was my notebook. It was the one thing I had that was irreplaceable; the one thing I needed to make the next part of my journey happen.

At once, every sinew and electron of my existence became laser focused on one thing—laying my hands upon one standard-issue reporter's notebook, rectangular, 8 inches by four inches, with ruled paper and a metal spiral binding at the top. On my last official day as a full-time employee at the *Post*, I'd stopped by the copy aide station, where my journey into the fraternity of journalists had begun as a 21-year-old law school dropout. Finding myself alone, perhaps overcome with emotion, I grabbed several dozen notebooks from the office supplies cabinet and stuffed them into my backpack. Though I'm sure I didn't know the word at the time, I think I considered the notebooks a kind of severance (even thought it was I who decided to leave, it wasn't like anybody jumped in my path and urged me to please stay). Or maybe I just needed something talismanic to bridge me over as I entered my uncertain future as a freelance writer. For so many years, my name had been "Mike Sager from the *Washington Post*." Stripped of my affiliation, I was only me, some guy nobody had ever heard of.

Drops of cold sweat ran down my ribcage, I pulled my backpack out from underneath the seat in front of me and into my lap, the way I've just done in Jeff's car. Anxiously I opened the inside zipper pocket, the place I always store my hallowed pads.

And of course, there it was.

Because I come from a long line of anxious worriers and I always check and recheck things a million times . . .

(Which doesn't make a bit of difference, as you might know.)

For the next thirty minutes, I soothed and reoriented myself as one must do after such an episode, flipping the pages of the notebook one by one, not so much reading as gazing, as one might scroll through photos of a fond and just-concluded vacation.

Right as I drifted off to sleep, *I put the notebook in my seatback pocket.*

As if by miracle Jeff's truck makes it across all six lanes of traffic and we catch the next exit, Sunset Boulevard. We find a gas station. At the convenience store I get a bunch of quarters. Without much discussion, we grab a pair of pay phone booths and start looking up numbers in the provided Yellow and White Pages—and just like that the old team is back in action.

Standing at our respective phones, receivers cradled between shoulders and ears, we take a moment for a fist bump. "We got this," Jeff says.

I'm not so sure.

A short time later, we find ourselves at a garbage facility behind the airport. With a little help from another of my nifty *Post* business cards, I earn the ear of a desk clerk. After some some polite and self-deprecating pleading, she consents to look up my flight. That we are able to get to this stage bespeaks the time period.

Back then, as now, an important element of your journalistic chops has to do with your ability to *finagle* your way through a problem—to say and do the things, make the contacts, and comport yourself in a way that induces your source or other gatekeeper to allow access to the things you need to carry out your mission. Today, there are a lot more obstacles in your way. In order to avoid liability, all segments of life are governed by strict standards and practices.

Be that as it may, this is all true. The clerk listens, takes pity, and consents to consult her logbook. By some miracle—perhaps my particular choices along this journey have earned me some karma?—the truck transporting the trash *from my particular flight* is just coming through the gates of the facility. On the downside, the load is a mixture of several flights, *including* mine. There is no way of knowing which bag is which.

Out the back door is a vast asphalt parking lot. As far as the eye can see there are industrial-size trash bags, both paper and plastic. Presumably this is a transshipment point, I don't want to ask any more questions, I'm only here for one thing. Standing on the back steps of the pre-fab office building, we watch as the truck with the trash from my flight is directed by a workman to dump his load.

After the truck pulls away, we are escorted across the lot to the site and provided with a supervisor.

A true partner, Jeff throws himself into the job alongside me. We go through the bags barehanded. As each bag is untied and carefully unpacked onto the ground, our supervisor stands like a stone at parade rest, a distasteful look on his face. Once each bag's contents are searched, we repack, re-tie, and set it aside.

We fall into a rhythm. Untie. Unpack, stir, repack, retie. Every few minutes, another jet takes off; there is a flight path directly over our heads. Each departure rips open the sky, creating thunderous vibrations that rumble the ground and rise through the souls of our feet, filling and surrounding us inside and out, deafening us, taking our breaths away, an invisible micro cataclysm. Taken together with the smell of the thousands of bags of garbage that are collected here in this huge, fenced, asphalt lot, conditions are difficult. Jeff and I take to pulling our shirts up over our noses. I feel jetlagged—that queasy, nauseous, really-need-to-lay-down kind of feeling.

Time passes. An hour? Two? We press on. We go through three jumbo jets worth of bags. "A shit ton," Jeff jokes at some point.

A wide range of slap-happy potty humor proceeds. No matter how you cut it, with the high fences and all the turd-shaped bags of trash arrayed around us—and the goodly number of used baby diapers in evidence in the bags contributing to an indescribable smell—it does feel as if we're kind of metaphorically, if not actually, inside the bowl of a big toilet in desperate need of a flush.

(As it turns out, it will be a good prelude to our next trip, to meet the exiled Bikini Islanders in a place where the latrines are hand dug and the rats are as plentiful, and as visible, as the birds.)

With the sun setting, there are only two bags left.

And no notebook. Not yet.

Maybe they're wrong about which load of trash this is?

I mean, sure, I can always call Cynthia long distance and ask for the contacts again. But how would that look? I'm trying to gain Marlon's trust and respect, aren't I? *Excuse me, I lost my notebook on the plane.* Not a good look, Mr. *Washington Post* journalist.

Just then, I find a boarding pass from the *same row in which I was sitting.*

Willy-nilly, I empty out the remaining contents of the bag, making an arc across the asphalt. (A skid mark?)

Holy shit. There it is.

There it is!

There it fucking is.

In the next-to-last bag. (This is the absolute truth. Honest to fucking God. Jeff was there. He'll back me up. He even took a photograph.)

I am so relieved I begin to sob.

Jeff pats my shoulder and makes another poopy joke.

***

The first thing I do when we arrive at Jeff's parents' house is use the phone.

Pat Quinn is Marlon's personal assistant. She is *one degree of separation* from my objective. She's been with Marlon for twenty years.

Pat, I will later learn, is a retired actress. She played Alice in the classic movie *Alice's Restaurant,* adapted from the 1967 folk song "Alice's Restaurant Massacree," originally written and sung by Arlo Guthrie.

The first try, nobody answers.

I wait sixty seconds, an eternity, watching the sweep second hand on my watch, remembering to breathe.

When I call back the second time, she answers.

I introduce myself and do an abridged version of my Cynthia speech.

"I'm so glad you loved Teti'aroa," she says pleasantly. "I was expecting your call. I'll phone Marlon today, or tomorrow at the latest," she promises.

***

For the next three days, I sprawl on the bed in the guest room at Jeff's parents' house, flipping channels. In a few years' time, there will be a song by Bruce Springsteen called "57 Channels (And Nothing On)."

It is already true.

Every time the house phone rings, I sit at attention and attune my ear, waiting for Armony to call my name.

After lunch on each successive day, I drive up the hill in my rental car, from Sherman Oaks to Marlon's place on Mulholland Drive, a serpentine two-lane that slithers east and west across the summit of the Mulholland Mountains. To the north is the San Fernando Valley, the land of aspirations. To the south is Hollywood, the land of dreams come true.

Marlon's compound is guarded at the entrance by a massive iron fence. Concertina wire is looped characteristically along the top; there are three cameras in view; the provided squawk box has two buttons but no names listed. Marlon is known to share the gate and the driveway with fellow acting icon Jack Nicholson, his co-star in the movie *The Missouri Breaks*.

Mulholland Drive is only 2 lanes in most spots and narrow; the terrain is steep; at some places you can see out over both sides at once. Motorcycle deaths are a frequent occurrence. I slow down and pull into Marlon's driveway.

After a quick look around, I back out perilously and drive a few hundred feet, to a convenient scenic turnout on the same side of the road as Marlon's place. There are no houses in between. Miraculously, through the bare winter trees, I can clearly see what must be his property—a low-slung compound of modest buildings on a little rise overlooking the gate.

As I did on his island, at his compound there, I take some time to sit a while and share Marlon's vista, to see what he sees. In this case, the breathtaking views are of Benedict Canyon, and the city of Los Angeles beyond.

I sit with the engine running, smoke a couple of cigarettes, watch his property for signs of movement. He's close, real close. I can feel him sucking me in even as I can feel him repelling me.

But I don't linger.

What if he's calling the house this very minute?

***

By day five, I can't stand it any longer.

I call Pat.

No answer.

I leave a message after the beep.

I call three more times.

I leave three more messages.

***

Pat answers on day six.

"Hi! How are you?" I ask, keeping it light.

"I cannot converse with you." Her voice is ice.

"What about the interview? What about—"

"I'm sorry, Mr. Sager. I am not at liberty to converse with you in any fashion."

The line goes dead.

I am not at liberty to converse with you in any fashion?

What the hell is that? Some kind of legal boilerplate?

After all this time? All this way? All my efforts large and small to comport myself as a decent human being?

Fucking *boilerplate?*

I thought I was in, didn't you?

***

Three more days pass.

Unaccountably, there is more rain. (I thought it never rained in sunny California. Am I being followed by a black cloud?)

More channel surfing. More fretting. Jeff's dad, Jack, the therapist, turns me on to his old-school-style wood hot tub. In some ways he reminds me of that character on the TV show M.A.S.H, B.J. Honeycutt. He's lanky and super smart and laid back, and just the right amount of perverse. We go after dark, when the sky is clear and the air is crisp. It feels kind of like being in bed on a cold morning, in a cold room, covered up to your neck by a warm blanket, all cozy. With the glow of suburbia polluting the darkness, there are not as many stars visible as on Teti'aroa, but there are still a lot.

I call Marlon's other assistant, Aiko. Cynthia had given me her number as a backup to Pat. She doesn't respond.

I call a woman in Los Angeles I'd met on Teti'aroa. She once worked for the music mogul Quincy Jones. Quincy has been to Teti'aroa. He's friends with Marlon. Maybe he has some way in?

I call my old frat brother. His father knows someone who knows someone who once had Marlon to dinner at his house. We catch up on college gossip. He promises to work that angle for me.

I call Cynthia in Tahiti.

"Mr. Sager! Hello! You are well?"

Cynthia sounds genuinely glad to hear from me. I tell her what's happened with Pat and she sounds surprised. "Wow, I don't know what to think about that," she says.

"Marlon has a lot of problems right now," she says, measuring her words.

I thank Cynthia. She wishes me luck. She's trying to sound upbeat, but I've heard plenty of friendly-sounding kiss-offs before.

At this point, I've been hunting Marlon Brando for months—at home in the dark in my living room; in the hallowed halls of the Library of Congress; in a smudged little mirror. On jets and planes; in taxis and tuk-tuks; through monsoon rains; at an expensive beach resort; through the restless jungle; even in a dugout canoe. During all that time, I've had zero contact with any personal friends besides Jeff. I haven't worked on any other stories or proposals. I have a monthly column at the local magazine back in Washington. It is due. I haven't written it yet. I haven't even called my sister or my parents. The last they heard, I was off to Tahiti to hunt for Marlon Brando.

The only thing that matters anymore is meeting Marlon.

Interviewing him. Hanging out with him. Picking his brain— and maybe a musical interlude with guitar and congas? We could play the songs I learned from Matahi. I'm sure he knows them.

It was a crazy assignment, I know. But I agreed to do it. And I cannot rest until I look Marlon in the eyes, hear his voice, see him walk across a room toward me and shake my hand, which is still deeply tanned from my time on his sunny, idyllic atoll.

***

An idea pops into my mind.

The Hail Mary.

I go to Radio Shack, a once-ubiquitous corner electronics store, and buy a small tape recorder, an analog device designed to capture sound on exchangeable 4" by 2" magnetic cassette tapes.

From there I head up to Mulholland Drive. I park in the scenic turnout that shares Marlon's view.

I pull out a cassette tape of Tahitian songs I'd bought at one of the souvenir shops at Faa'a Airport and insert it into the tape deck in my rental car. As the music begins to issue forth from the speakers, I push the button on the tape recorder.

"Dear Mr. Brando. Please forgive this further intrusion." The little sprockets turn. I feel breathless, as if I've been running. My voice quavers.

"In the several months I've spent learning about you, visiting Teti'aroa, and meeting your extended family, I have become a true admirer. I flatter only the facts when I conclude you are a man with great vision. I am aware you have chosen to voluntarily withdraw from dealings with the greater world, but the situation on our planet has become dire. I believe sincerely your ideas and experience are needed to help the world.

"What I am offering is this: A 10,000-word article in the *Washington Post Sunday Magazine*. One million copies of the magazine are distributed every week. You can direct the subject matter. Any cause or concern. The choice is yours. I will be your willing conduit.

"I know you must have gotten reports from your people concerning my handling of this assignment. As you might be aware, during all of my time on Teti'aroa, I took no pictures of your family.

I did not intrude. I did not act at all like the typical sort of journalist you have so long despised, and for good reason. Instead, I acted with all possible respect. To treat as I would be treated.

"I know you want to be left alone. But I also know you care about the world and about doing good things. I know you're an idealist—or at least you were at one time. The world is suffering. If we act now, maybe we can help." My voice cracks; I'm getting a little carried away. The song playing on the car's stereo system is a traditional Polynesian folk ballad. The music wells into expansive chorus of harmonious voices that breaks upon the shoreline of my pitiful state.

Slowly and clearly, I twice recite the phone number at Armony and Jack's place. Then thank him for his time and click the stop button.

I put the tape recorder, along with some copies of my past stories—about the Great Peace March for Global Nuclear Disarmament; the new and unsettling trend of urine testing employees for drugs; and a profile of a Native American icon named Princess Pale Moon—into a one gallon-size Ziploc baggie. I've chosen the baggie because it seals, and also because Marlon can easily see there's no bomb or other harmful material inside.

***

I pull into Marlon's driveway and stop in front of the ten-foot iron gate. Cyclone fencing continues into the treeline on either side. The sky is very blue today, washed clean by the seasonal winds. The razors on the concertina glint in the bright winter sunlight. A security camera on the fence informs me I'm under surveillance. There's also a red sign that promises "Armed Response."

I press both buttons on the intercom. There seems to be a camera inside there, too.

After a few moments, the box squawks: "Yes?"

"Package for Mr. Brando." I wave toward the cameras, *hello*.

The gate begins to creak open.

"Drive slowly and take the left fork."

The asphalt road reminds me a bit of the airstrip on Teti'aroa; weathered and patched. The road climbs upward through a densely wooded area. When I reach the fork, I follow directions. I figure the right fork leads to Nicolson's place. I don't know it now, but one day, decades hence, Nicholson will invite me to his house to conduct an interview for a cover story for *Esquire*. I'll drive through this very gate and take the right fork. By then, Marlon will no longer be around.

The road peters out in front of a dense green hedgerow, at least twenty feet tall. I figure the plants are fake. They're just too green and perfect to be real?

I sit a moment with my foot on the brake, trying to be patient, remembering to breathe. I look around and try to see what I can see, which is not much, hemmed in as I am on all sides by the forest.

As I'm sitting there, a fault line appears in the hedgerow. The gap grows larger as the shrubs retreat to either side . . .

Revealing a gravel and asphalt parking area. I drive forward and kill the engine.

The compound is not at all grand, reminiscent of the one I found in Teti'aroa, a gathering of bungalows with a common area in between. Instead of coconut wood and woven fronds, the buildings have more conventional windows and are constructed of stucco.

A sign advises: "Stay in Car. Attack Dogs on Premises."

***

A young man appears.

He is handsome and well-muscled, wearing jeans and a white T-shirt. He's being led by a Doberman on a leash.

I am struck dumb.

It's Stanley Kowalski—*Stella!*

It's Terry Malloy—*I coulda been a contenda!*

It's Johnny Strabler, leader of the Strebler Black Rebels Motorcycle Club, riding into Carbonville, California, and causing a heap of trouble.

"What are you rebelling against, Johnny?"

"Whaddaya got?"

Turned-down lips, chiseled jaw, high cheekbones, tousled hair. Marlon in his prime, Marlon when he was turning Hollywood upside down. Long before all the wives and press and politics and bullshit drove him away from the world.

Only *this* Marlon has light brown skin, almond-shaped eyes, and tawny hair. Just like his sister, Cheyenne.

Images of my time in Teti'aroa come flooding back. Digging my feet into the warm sand on the beach, floating like a hippo in the lagoon, hanging out beneath the stars, the fire crackling, singing and playing the guitar. I am nearly overcome with emotions.

I shout out the window as if greeting a long-lost friend (in the style of the day): "Teihotu! What's happenin', man!"

Marlon's son appears taken aback. *Why is this delivery guy calling me by name? I could be a be psycho, you never know.* I'm sure Marlon gets plenty of them. The dog growls and bares its teeth, pulls at its leash.

"How can I help you?" Teihotu says.

I introduce myself and mention Cynthia.

"She said you might be coming." His words are neither warm nor cold. He issues a command and the Doberman sits.

"Teri'i told me to say hello," I say. "He wants to know when you're coming back. He just harvested the crop. It was pretty *skunky.* Oh, and I'm supposed to tell you Charles and Popi say . . ."

I am yammering away like a fool, but I can't help it.

Jesus fucking Christ, the kid looks *exactly* like his father.

At last, I manage to clamp my mouth shut. I can't tell *what* Teihotu is thinking. I thrust my arm out the open driver's window. From my hand dangles the one-gallon freezer baggie with the tape recorder, my message, my *Post* business card, and my clips.

"Can you please ask your dad (*Holy shit! Your DAD!*) to listen to this tape I made for him and think about my offer? This is really an amazing opportunity for him to help the world."

Without hesitation, Teihotu steps forward and takes the baggie from my hand. He doesn't seem the least bit suspect of the contents. I take it as a positive sign.

***

Three more days pass. There is no word from Marlon—not yet.

On the fourth day, I wake up in a complete and utter state of self-loathing. I'm not exactly sure what day it is; I have no idea how long I've been in California. I have set my watch and my calendar to Marlon. He is my only measure of time.

I feel like a total idiot.

I will never make anything of myself but a laughingstock.

First, I quit law school. Even a government lawyer makes six figures a year. Then I quit the *Post*, one of the most esteemed news-gathering organizations in the world. Now I'm hunting Marlon Brando? This is me being true to my art? Seeing how far I can go?

Propped on two pillows in the guest bed, in the bright and prom-ising light of a sunny morning, with the river-rush of distant freeway traffic and winter birdsong filling the air, it becomes clear to me this entire hopeless charade has turned out to be a bad idea, an error in judgment worse even than my first marriage, which seemed wholly *brilliant* at the time—a little less than a year ago now—a somewhat spontaneous event celebrated at the office of the justice of the peace in the city of Roadtown, Tortola, in the British Virgin Islands, on the very same day the space shuttle Challenger broke apart 73 seconds after launch, killing all seven crew members. We were together a total of six months. It will take a year to get divorced. Talk about expensive winter vacations.

As this story is in danger of becoming.

Expensive on so many levels—financial, professional, physical, psychotherapeutic. The only reason I left the house yesterday was to drive to the pharmacy to get more antacids. I think I'm devel-oping an ulcer. Or irritable bowel syndrome. My heart keeps doing flip flops. I'm only 30 but I'm a little worried I'm having a heart attack, or warning signs of a heart attack, or maybe not an *attack* but some kind of trouble. (It will be decades before I become wise to the nefarious manipulations wreaked upon your body by demon anxiety, or even the fact that anxiety is an actual diagnosis, and not just a natural condition of my Jewish upbringing.)

To hell with Marlon Brando.

To hell with *hunting* Marlon Brando.

No editor at the *Washington Post*, even madcap Jay Lovinger with his fucking Mona Lisa tie, is going to give Marlon Brando 10,000 words in which to ramble at will. And who the fuck cares about his opinion, anyway? What could he possibly have to say that will help the world? Sure, he's had great instincts about using his fame as a platform for social change, but at the end of the day, he's nothing but an actor. A pretty person who is incredibly good at playing pretend. Why am I chasing him across the globe?

Maybe actors should just act, singers sing, ballers ball. Why do we even need to know everything about their lives and what they're thinking and what their opinions might be? That's not what they're being paid for, is it?

I swing my feet to the floor, take stock of my accommodations. A sewing machine sits on top of the desk—a basket of mending occupies the chair. A Barbie Club House belonging to one of the granddaughters hunkers to one side of the room, blocking entrance to the closet.

I throw on sweatpants, shoes, and a hoodie, open the sliding glass door, and step into the back yard. A few feet away is another Barbie Club House, this one big enough to accommodate actual children.

Stooping down, I venture inside the pink plastic structure and take a seat on one of the two kindergarten-size chairs. Out of my pocket comes an airtight plastic film can containing the last crumbs of Marlon's marijuana. I roll a joint and smoke. Then I sit for a very long time, staring at my distorted face in the toy mirror hanging over the faux fireplace, taking stock.

At this point I've devoted more than three months to Marlon. I've flown over 10,000 miles. I've spent all my expense money allotted for both stories on this contract, and I've yet to buy my plane ticket for the second piece, which could actually be something impactful and newsworthy . . . if I would ever go down there and do it.

I always knew this would be an impossible assignment. Everyone I'd consulted had advised me to turn it down—too risky, they all said, you're going to fail, it's a can't-win situation, you're setting yourself up for a fall.

But I took the job anyway because I wanted to stretch myself, to raise my game. I wanted to do *more* than just a story. I wanted to write something big and important and lasting. Something epic. Something meaningful. Something that would seal my reputation. Change the conversation. Maybe even get me a movie deal.

As it was, this big shot editor suggested a hunt for Marlon Brando, the most elusive actor of our time.

And I agreed.

And now I have to finish what I started.

***

I take a fresh razor to my head, shower and dress.

I leave Jeff's parents' house, drive to the local market and buy bagels, a large coffee, two newspapers, a couple of waters, some snacks, two packs of cigarettes, an extra Bic lighter. Riding past a sporting goods store, I have a lightbulb moment; I run inside and buy a decent pair of 10x50 binoculars. Then I make my way up to the heights of Mulholland Drive. I park at the scenic overlook with the view of Marlon's compound.

And just like that, I am no longer a decent human being on a mission to do good (while meanwhile enhancing my own reputation).

Instead, I'm just another asshole reporter desperate for a previously unreported tidbit to write into the lede of a rehashed story about Marlon Brando's life.

But dammit, that is exactly what I need. I'd been trained by the best. I know what is required. Some *bang-bang* footage. Something live. Something to justify myself and my assignment. And all the money I've spent.

Sitting in my car at the overlook, scanning Marlon's compound with the binoculars, I try again to summon the Method. To channel the Marlon I've watched and studied and dreamed about. At this point I'm so stressed and desperate I don't even need the hard drugs.

I'm a contender. I'm a young lion. I'm a wild one. I'm an eyeball in a cave: *The horror! The horror!* I'm a factory parts salesman living in an upstairs apartment in the humid, working-class Faubourg Marigny neighborhood of New Orleans with his wife, Stella DuBois Kowalski. I am Zapata, I am Caesar, I am motherfuckin' Don Corleone.

The sky is gray and cloudy. Predatory hawks soar over the canyon, hunting for rats and snakes and other small creatures. Cars screech around the curves of Mulholland Drive. Packs of motorcycles rumble by. What they see is a guy in a subcompact rental car, wearing a black Nikon baseball-style cap, looking through a big-ass pair of binoculars into somebody's private property.

I know what they think.

I'm thinking it about myself, too.

In *Last Tango in Paris*, Marlon plays an aging hotel owner mourning the suicide of his wife. He begins a raw, anonymous sexual relationship with a young, Parisian woman played by Maria Schneider. At one point during the film, Marlon tells her, "In order to live your life, you have to look first into the maw of death."

Sitting at this scenic overlook in this budget rental car, squinting through this brand new pair of binoculars, I think I understand.

Four hours pass. In real life I can never sit still for this long. But when I'm working I am flooded with some kind of hormone, perhaps linked to the primitive hunters who were our ancestors, that allows me to be still and do nothing—except observe—for exceedingly long periods of time. It's as if, because I'm engaged to do a job, I have superhuman focus. Luckily, at this point of my life I am young and do not yet have to pee as often as I will someday.

As I spy on Marlon's compound, I listen to my tapes of Tahitian music. I think about Teri'i and Popi and the other folks on Marlon's island. I think about Angelina. I wonder again what exactly went down with her, why she so abruptly left the island. Had it been something to do with the gynecological problems she'd confided about during our very first meeting? I wish I had more answers. I wish I had more of Marlon's weed.

And then . . . at some point during hour five . . . I detect movement.

I rub my eyes and look again.

Up there, through a break in the tree line, one hundred yards away, on a deck that seems to connect two of the bungalows in Marlon's compound . . .

I raise the binoculars.

It's Teihotu. Clear as day.

With the 10x50 binocs, one hundred yards appears to be ten yards away. It looks as if he's no more than thirty feet from me.

The binoculars want to bob and sway, making it hard to maintain a bead on my target. I rest the barrels on the steering wheel for stability. I hold my breath like they teach in all the sniper movies.

Teihotu is carrying a typical garden-variety hand saw. In the other hand he's balancing a long piece of lumber; I'm guessing it's a two-by-six, a typical size used for decking.

And then . . . following along behind . . .

Holy shit.

There he is!

Marlon fucking Brando.

I dial the focus wheel to get a sharper look.

Marlon is fat. *Hugely fat.* He's wearing a blue bathrobe. He looks tired and worried. He is bald on top with a tangled fringe of white hair on the sides. He points here, points there, gives directions.

It's been thirteen years since he made *Godfather* and earned his second Oscar, which he refused to accept, and about $21 million in salary and back end percentages, which he did accept. Next came *Last Tango, The Missouri Breaks, Superman, Apocalypse Now,* and *The Formula.* For the last three, in total, he was seen on screen for less than 30 minutes. He was paid more than $10 million each.

With the binoculars I can see Marlon pretty clearly. He's one football field away. If my scenic turnout is one end zone, his compound is the other.

I see nothing of the Brat, the Slob, the Valentino of the Bop Generation, the Walking Hormone Factory, the man standing alone far away, the visionary.

I see nothing of Terry Malloy, Stanley Kowalski, Fletcher Christian. I see nothing of the groundbreaking actor and activist, nothing of the template for the modern American male.

All I see is an old guy. Fat and bald with flyaway hair, wearing a blue bathrobe in the middle of the afternoon, directing his son to repair his deck.

I watch for a while. There is much discussion. There is measuring and sawing and hammering. Another board is retrieved, and then another.

I've been hunting Marlon now for three months. I copied his pictures and taped them to my walls. I read every book and every article, watched every movie several times. I even transcribed the dialogue on my laptop. (If you're a big fan, you might detect some of that dialogue sprinkled through this narrative, quoted as a jazz player might quote a familiar song in a solo.)

I dropped down deep, very deep, into my own kind of Method—in his wife I saw an old girlfriend; in his divorce I saw my soon-to-be-ex-wife; in his art I found a meaning; in his vision I saw a better future. I saw a snail crawl along the edge of a straight razor. Crawling, slithering, along the edge of a straight razor . . . and surviving. That was my dream. That was my nightmare. I knew beyond a doubt that someday I'd return.

And now—sitting in my little rental car at this scenic overlook, watching Marlon through the binoculars—something occurs to me, obvious but no less startling: For the first time in three months, I know Marlon's *exact* location.

As if in a trance, I key the ignition, the car putters to life. I drive down the hill to his driveway and turn in.

I stop at the imposing gate he shares with his buddy Nicholson. I edge up to the little intercom box.

As before, I push both buttons—I don't know which of the two is which.

Just as I do, a car comes into view, descending the hill from the direction of Marlon's compound. It's a Toyota. It pulls to a stop on the other side of the gate, mirroring my position.

Slowly, the gate opens inward, away from me.

As it's moving, a woman emerges from the car. She's fortyish, Japanese. I know instantly who it is—it's got to be Aiko, Marlon's other personal assistant.

After Pat had told me she "couldn't converse," I'd called Aiko.

Teri'i also knew Aiko. "Japan lady. Very smart. Make much organized. Good!"

Whatever. She declined to return any of my thirteen calls.

Now Aiko walks through the gate, crosses in front of my car, toward the mailbox, which is located on the opposite side of the driveway from the ringer and squawk box. Although I am sitting right here, behind the wheel with the motor running, she totally ignores me.

She opens the box. She stands for a few moments as people will do, sorting through the mail.

I lean across the passenger seat and roll down the window. "Aiko?"

She turns toward me. She acts kind of startled, as if she hadn't noticed me there.

"I'm Mike Sager. You know. From the *Washington Post?*"

"How are you today?" she asks.

How do you fucking think I am?

"I was wondering if Marlon received my package," I say sheepishly.

"Why yes, of course!" she says, stepping a step closer, putting on a saccharin smile. "We *forwarded* it to Marlon at his *next stop*. I'm not at liberty to say where he's going. But he's not here anymore. I'm sure he'll get back to you on the matter very soon. I'm sure it will all work out . . ."

Her lips are moving, but I'm not hearing any sound.

This bitch is lying to my face.

I have just seen Marlon Brando. He is fat and bald, wearing a blue bathrobe. He's up there on his deck.

I have traveled 10,000 miles. Spent thousands. Staked my career. *Give me a fucking break?*

I look at Aiko. She's maybe ten feet away. Marlon is no more than 30 feet away, behind a fence and up a hill and through the thickly wooded area to my left.

And then I look toward the gate. It is fully open. Aiko's car is in front of mine, sort of blocking me. But with my subcompact, I estimate, there is plenty of room to squeeze thorough.

I could floor it right now. I could be in Marlon's compound in a few seconds. It's right up the driveway. I've been there before. Even if I have to climb over the fancy camouflaged gate, I'll get in.

Even if someone calls the police, it'll take least fifteen minutes for them to arrive. Probably more. Mulholland is narrow. There are lots of tourists lollygagging along. *By then I could find Marlon and get a quote!*

One quote. At the very least. One live quote to show I found him.

Like a game of capture the flag, I just need to steal a few words and run back to base.

If they want to arrest me on my way out, fine. There's my ending. I get arrested and hauled away.

Or maybe . . .

Maybe, once I get inside the compound, (and use the leftover bagels to distract the Dobermans?) Marlon will be impressed with my monumental efforts to track him down. Maybe he'll see my dedication and consider me a fellow artist—a person, like himself, who is fully committed to the service of his work, and to the greater work of living life.

Maybe, before the cops get here, we'll have time to become acquainted a bit.

Time to become—dare I say? *Friends?*

I mean, I'm not just a fucking reporter. I carried Tarita's fish. Marlon's people fuckin' loved me. We made music together. We smoked weed.

Hadn't I refrained from taking exclusive pictures of Cheyenne as she sped through the jungle on the huge tractor? Did I mention how beautiful she was? Did I mention she'd been topless? No, I didn't. I wrote earlier she was wearing a bikini because I wanted to be respectful of Marlon's daughter and her beautiful but private anatomy.

Hadn't I refrained from crow-barring open Marlon's private residence? I could have been all up inside his room and his desk and his file cabinets and everything. What secrets did I turn down in order to stay right with the universe?

Right with Him.

In *Apocalypse Now*, before Captain Willard goes up the river, the general tries to prepare him for his unique and difficult mission. "You see, Willard," the general says, "things get confused out there. Power, ideals, morality . . . there's a conflict in every human heart between the rational and the irrational, between good and evil."

Captain Willard, of course, was a soldier. An assassin. That was his job. In the movie he gets it done. You should see the final scenes. If you want, you should get high first. Or maybe not too high. It's pretty intense.

Of course, I'm not a soldier or hired assassin. I'm a journalist.

It's a strange profession, not unlike Willard's, although murder is not the aim. I try to maneuver myself behind the lines of people's inner lives and personalities. I take scrapings of their insides, samples of their deepest thoughts and feelings, and then I display my findings for everyone to see, hopefully in an evocative literary style.

I do all this under the banner of The People's Right to Know. I listen, I nod, I open my posture. I suss out what they need, say what they want to hear. I do what I have to do to get my story, just like Willard has to do in the movie to get his man.

But this time . . . I wanted it to be different.

I figured I could show myself to Marlon as a man worthy of meeting.

Not just a typical reporter; a decent human being.

But somewhere along the line, things became confused. Maybe I started believing my own con.

Unfortunately for me, Marlon is not confused. He knows better. He has always known better. He knows me better than I know myself. My oh-so-clever elevator pitch in a Ziploc baggie is never going to change his mind. He will never even open it. It will never be heard. I'm sure it went directly into the trash.

No matter how I try to parse it, or how perfectly I comport myself, I'm still just another journalist trying to write a story—albeit with good intentions. (Ha, don't we all say that?)

Aiko knows this all too well.

Which is why she's standing there, ten feet away, lying to my face. And why she feels justified.

And maybe that's also why she seems to be enjoying herself so fucking much.

Because to her, my face isn't just my face. It's the face of all journalists, of all the scoop slobs and news hounds and gossips and investigators who have hunted Marlon for thirty years—or however long she has been with him, probably forever like the others in his employ.

From the start it sounded ridiculous: "Go to Tahiti and find Marlon Brando."

And, from the start, I'd wondered: "What should I do once I find him?"

"You'll know," Lovinger had said. Everyone agreed he was one of the best editors in the business. When the *Washington Post* wanted to get serious about publishing a Sunday magazine, they'd looked far and wide and ended up choosing him. And he chose me.

I'll know?

I look at Aiko, standing by the mailbox, mocking me with her Mona Lisa smile like Lovinger's tie. *Is this all you've got, Sager.*

I take measure of the open space between the far bumper of Aiko's Toyota and the gate-pole. I'm pretty sure my vehicle will fit through, causing at the very most only minor damage. When I travel for work, I always take the extra insurance on the car, just in case.

I reach forward and jab the play button on the car stereo. Tahitian music bursts forth at a high volume—guitars and voices warbling harmonically, the sound of a million stars shimmering in the dark night sky over Marlon's atoll.

Then I grab the stick shift of my rental car—full as it is of all the wrappers and drink cans and newspapers and other flotsam and jetsam I've collected the last couple of weeks during the course of these ridiculous and fruitless stakeouts—and jam it into reverse.

I back out of Marlon's driveway, onto Mulholland Drive.

I take the next plane home.

EPILOGUE

As I write this, nearly four decades have passed.

When I last saw Marlon, in December 1987, with the aid of a hastily purchased pair of 10x50 binoculars, he was 64 years old—fat, bald, distracted, dressed in a blue bathrobe, puttering around with his son at his compound on Mulholland Drive.

Today I'm 64.

Marlon has been dead for 16 years.

To my knowledge, our intersection had zero influence on the course of his life.

But for me, it changed everything.

***

The original title of my article was *Last Tango in Tahiti*. It was published in the *Washington Post Magazine* on Sunday, July 5, 1987. The cover illustration was an airbrushed, super-realistic depiction of Marlon peering out hauntedly from a deep shadow behind a palm frond, sunlight striping his face. It was painted by the artist Stan Watts.

Soon after the story ran, I contacted Watts and bought the cover illustration for $1,800. (For my story, the *Post* paid a fee of $2,750. I still have the contract. By some miracle I retained the rights. I no longer have copies of my expense invoice, which I recall included the expenses from two stories and totaled something in the neighborhood of $12,000.) The painting has been with me ever since, looking down from the wall in my office.

At nearly 14,000 words, *Last Tango in Tahiti* was long by any magazine standards of that era or this, at least three times the typical length of a long feature story, raising hackles across the *Post* newsroom, where word counts were a frequent battleground (especially during the print era when the space was finite).

It didn't help that I was a former *Post* staffer who'd chosen to leave the "golden handcuffs" of full-time employment three years earlier.

Or that I'd been sent, during the late fall and winter months, on an extended, all-expenses-paid trip to Tahiti, Hawaii, and California (and the Marshall Islands for story number two).

Or that I didn't actually complete the mission.

He went all that way, spent all that money, wrote all those words . . . and never even interviewed Marlon Brando!

Many dismissed the story as a boondoggle, one in a series of creative choices at the new magazine, executed on Jay Lovinger's watch, that offended sensibilities around Washington, a decidedly blue blazer-and-khaki pants kind of town. Eventually, Lovinger was let go by the *Post*. He took his Mona Lisa tie and returned to the New York magazine scene from whence he had come, where he continued his long and stellar career as a beloved and decorated editor, principally at the juggernaut ESPN.

(During the extended process of re-crafting this story, Lovinger passed away. I feel fortunate I was in touch with him and his family during his last days, especially his wife Gay Daly—an estimable author I have had the privilege to publish and to call my friend. He'd been in ill health but was seemingly on the upswing when he suddenly died. As it happened, I was scheduled to call him a few days hence—to catch up and to ask some questions about the Marlon assignment. Of course, there is a lesson here about putting off calls to people we cherish. In the absence of his voice, I dedicate to him this renovated version of our story and thank him once again for the plum assignment. Throughout my career I have been blessed by great assignments, served up by generous editors. I can never thank them enough. For their confidence in me I have always tried my hardest to honor them with my very best work.)

Even as I was in the throes of my obsessive hunt for Marlon Brando, I was enough in possession of my senses to realize it was all a silly game I was allowing myself to act out. I knew the story needed a sense of drama, so perhaps I allowed myself to get a little carried away with the "mission." It was also a good excuse, in the early days of the process, to allow myself the luxury of going a bit overboard with mind-altering substances.

All of which, looking back, was fun and relatively harmless, and hurt nobody, and made for good entertainment, which is what a story should do, no matter how long or short it is.

Except for one thing.

The part that became, over time, the core message of the piece, my thesis, echoed throughout:

Marlon hates the press. If I'm ever going to win his cooperation, I can't act like a typical journalist. I have to act like a decent human being.

When I came up with that—first as a refrain inside my mind, and later refined in type—it wasn't just because it sounded good.

(Though obviously it became my reportorial gambit—which Marlon knew better than I . . . to the extent he was aware of any of this insanity. I've never turned up any evidence that he read my story, or even that he'd been aware of my pursuit.)

Aided perhaps by my over-the-top, Method-based approach to this story—the Method employs deep empathy and no little bit of Stockholm Syndrome to speed actors to the place they need to be to inhabit a part—what happened was this: As my search for Marlon progressed, as I sized up my situation, I started to see things a little differently from the way I'd been trained at the *Washington Post*.

The foundation of newspaper journalism is objectivity—the objective reporting of events. But truly, life is too messy for the black and white of the objective, third-person omniscient reporter. Especially when you're trying to understand the *reasons* humans feel and do the things they do.

Yes, upon leaving the paper, I felt as if I had a lot to prove, as does any young person who leaves a fond home to seek their fortunes elsewhere. But to this day, I have great affection for the *Post*, for the people who taught me so much, and for the institution as a bastion of fact-based news gathering, a standard that seems to be slipping away amidst the social chaos of our present-day world. All I've managed to accomplish during my career is directly linked to the training (and no small amount of care) I received at the *Post* during my first six years of life as a professional journalist.

Nevertheless, my hunt for Marlon made me question and re-define my role as a writer and as a member of the press. Beginning with the Marlon story, the way I practiced journalism began to evolve. Everything I have written in these three decades since, every interaction with every person I have met (at work and in my personal life), everything I have taught students and younger writers, carries the DNA of the lessons I learned while doing this crazy story.

What came together in my mind while hunting Marlon was the notion that every interview is a privilege. The First Amendment we all talk about in the context of journalism has to do with freedom of expression (in the absence of legal malice); the ability of a free press to publish verified truth unimpeded. It has nothing to do with prying into people's private lives, which is really what you want to know, the ingredient that makes for the best stories, the deep true personal stuff.

Since my experience with Marlon, I no longer feel compelled to cast myself as I was trained, as an objective interrogator, probing my sources like a prosecutor or police detective for some kind of perceived absolute truth.

Instead, I've learned to comport myself a little more like a therapeutic anthropologist.

I listen carefully and sympathetically; suspend my disbelief; look beyond the actual syntax of the words being spoken in order to understand the actual intent. I try to put myself in the mindset of the speaker, in their body, in their soul—no matter how low down or guilty, no matter how different they are from me, no matter how much I disagree or am repulsed by the actual fact of what they might be saying or what they might have done.

Victim or perpetrator, famous or unknown—every person wants to be heard. Rarely do we realize that privilege: The full satisfaction of telling our story, from beginning to end, to someone willing to listen sympathetically, to someone willing to connect the dots as you do, to see from your point of view. This is what I try to do. And this is what I give back to my sources. It's not a lot but it's something to exchange for the privilege of using someone's life to make my art. In the end, it serves us both.

I think that's what Marlon would have wanted me to know.

***

Marlon died on July 1, 2004, at the age of 80, at the Ronald Reagan UCLA Medical Center. His eldest sister, Jocelyn, always an ally and a staunch supporter, was at his side. Initially, the cause of his death was withheld, his lawyer citing privacy concerns. Eventually the news was released: respiratory failure from pulmonary fibrosis with congestive heart failure. Marlon also suffered from diabetes and liver cancer.

(Marlon outlived his middle sister, Frances Brando Loving, who died in 1994, at the age of 71, in Mundelein, Lake County, Illinois. Little is known about her adult life; she left behind her long-time husband, Richard Loving. As you might recall, it had been Marlon's childhood pal, Wally Cox, who brought the couple together. Interestingly, Cox was also responsible for teaching metal work to Loving; in later years he would be lauded as an artist, particularly for his creations in silver. The Lovings had two sons. In *Songs My Mother Taught Me*, Marlon praises Frannie for going back to college in her 40s to become a teacher.)

A couple of months after his Marlon's death, a memorial was held at the house of his close friend and the co-executor of his will, producer Mike Medavoy. On hand with close friends and members of the family was an Olympian gathering of Hollywood OGs— Jack Nicholson, Warren Beatty, Sean Penn and others. Eventually, Marlon's ashes were comingled with ashes belonging to Cox, and also with ashes belonging to another longtime friend, Sam Gilman, whom Marlon and Cox befriended during their earliest years together in New York. Gilman is most remembered as the actor who plays Doc Holliday in a third season episode of *Star Trek: The Original Series*, "Spectre of the Gun." Gilman also had parts in a number of Marlon's movies, including *The Men* (uncredited, his first movie role), *The Wild One*, *Désirée*, *The Young Lions*, *One-Eyed Jacks*, and *The Missouri Breaks*.

A portion of the mixed cremains were scattered in Death Valley; the rest were sprinkled from the air over his beloved Teti'aroa.

Marlon's eldest sister, Jocelyn, known as Tiddy, died a little more than a year after Marlon, of natural causes at her Santa Monica home. Jocelyn was married twice, and had two sons, one with each husband. Her first husband was Don Hammer, an American film actor who started on Broadway, where he was once considered a big star. He later appeared in some 90 films between 1945 until 1991, in mostly small parts. Jocelyn's second husband was Eliot Asinof, a writer best known for *Eight Men Out*, a nonfiction reconstruction of the 1919 Black Sox professional baseball scandal, considered by journalists to be a memorable piece of sports writing.

Eventually, Jocelyn changed her surname to Pennebaker, Dodie's maiden name, and opened a bookstore in Santa Monica, The Book Bin. An avid poet, she conducted workshops at her home in the Intensive Journal method, a self-therapy technique since widely adopted.

In 2009, work began on The Brando resort, a new, ultra-luxury property built to replace the quaint, beach-side hotel I visited so many years ago on Teti'aroa.

The new place was constructed and is managed by Pacific Beachcomber, a large hotel and cruise operator in French Polynesia. The first phase of their makeover included reconstruction and reorientation of the runway to meet more current aviation regulations. In addition, a reef dock was built to enable the transfer of supplies from the ocean side of the reef to the lagoon side. The resort opened in July 2014. According to reports, the Brando estate and eight of Marlon Brando's eleven children are involved in the project.

The Brando is billed as a "unique luxury resort co-existing with a center for scientific research, education and conservation." The resort has 35 deluxe villas, each with its own private beach and plunge pool; a holistic spa; and "the unmatched service and hospitality of the Polynesian people." The resort also reports having on site a "Green Leader" and a "Green Team"—a group of hotel staff members, including a Pacific Beachcomber marine biologist/

veterinarian, charged with "activating ideas to conserve and protect the environment."

According to the website, The Brando project works in concert with the Teti'aroa Society, which acts as the environmental steward of the atoll, with the authority and responsibility to "manage, conserve and protect, and preserve the natural beauty, biodiversity and cultural heritage of Teti'aroa Atoll through ongoing scientific research, education and community engagement." Carrying out their work in the name of Marlon and his descendants, the resort and the society say they are working together to become "a global model for sustainable travel, rooted in innovation and conservation, working to protect the planet for future generations."

After his presidency ended, in early 2017, Barack Obama stayed at The Brando for an entire month. He was said to be spending part of his time working on his presidential memoirs.

According to published rates, a one-bedroom villa at The Brando goes for $3,000 to $5,000 per person per night, depending upon the time of year.

***

Looking back, Marlon's acting career spanned 60 years. He won two Academy Awards for Best Actor.

The first came in 1954, for his portrayal of Terry Malone, a young boxer convinced to take a fall in *On the Waterfront*. His famous line from the movie, "I coulda been a contender," is still current in the cultural lexicon.

His second Oscar was awarded in 1973, for his role as Vito Corleone in *The Godfather*, one of the most memorable film characters of all time. (Though he refused to show up to receive his gold statue, he is still the winner of record.)

Marlon also received Oscar nominations for playing Emiliano Zapata in *Viva Zapata!*; Mark Antony in Joseph L. Mankiewicz's film adaptation of Shakespeare's *Julius Caesar* (1953); Air Force Major Lloyd Gruver in *Sayonara*, an adaptation of the James Michener novel;

the American widower Paul in *Last Tango in Paris*; and lawyer Ian McKenzie in *A Dry White Season* (1989).

Random-seeming as it might be, the American Film Institute ranks Marlon as the fourth-greatest movie star among male movie stars whose screen debuts occurred in or before 1950. In 1998 he was named Actor of the Century by *Time*. The following year, he was one of only six artists and entertainers named to the magazine's list of the 100 Most Important People of the Century.

On a deeper level, Marlon's influence can be seen across the entire world. He is widely credited with being one of the first actors to bring the Stanislavski system of acting, and also Method Acting, derived from the Stanislavski system, to mainstream audiences, changing forever the way actors performed on film. All of today's actors have a at least a little bit of Marlon in their creative DNA.

Beyond acting, Marlon's persona, on and off screen, is said to have contributed to a change in the very notion of manhood in America. Before Marlon, the model American hero was embodied by actors like John Wayne and Kirk Douglas—swaggering, confident, loyal, honest, responsible, unwavering, unwilling to show feelings of any sort. Marlon became the archetype of a new kind of hero, the *anti-hero*, an ever-more complex male figure for ever-more complex times— conflicted, vulnerable, primitive, flawed, selfish, pansexual; an aesthete *living his own truth* long before anyone ever termed the expression.

Marlon's portrayal of the gang leader Johnny Strabler in *The Wild One* has become ubiquitous as both a symbol of rebelliousness and as a fashion statement: motorcycle jacket, tilted cap, jeans, white T-shirt, and sunglasses. At the time of the movie, Johnny's character inspired a worldwide craze for sideburns, a style picked up by James Dean and Elvis Presley . . . and pretty much all of the male population of the world. Dean copied Brando's acting style extensively; Presley used Brando's image as a model for his famous role in *Jailhouse Rock* (1957). In addition, according to cultural critic Linda Williams, "Brando was an early lesbian icon who, along with James Dean, influenced the butch look and self-image (among lesbians) in the 1950s and after."

Marlon was also a pioneer for celebrity activism at a time when celebrities were afraid to speak out, lest they be blackballed by big movie studios and derided by the movie-ticket-buying public.

He was among the earliest to raise the alarm about climate change. In 1994, on an episode of Larry King's talk show, Marlon disclosed that he'd signed with a company "designed to reduce the CO2 in the earth [in order] to preserve it for your grandchildren and for mine." In an otherwise rare, lighthearted interview, the septuagenarian Marlon turned serious: "Each one of us, everybody here in this room, sound, gaffers, assistants, we all have to do something to reverse the effects of the CO2."

Marlon's first arrest as a political activist came in March 1964, when he was taken into custody at a "fish-in" to protest Washington State fishing policies along the Puyallup River, near Mount Rainier, in a valley occupied for eons by members of the Puyallup Indian Tribe.

And, of course, there was his refusal to accept his *Godfather* Oscar in 1973, in protest of Hollywood's portrayal of Native Americans and to draw attention to the Standoff at Wounded Knee, when approximately 200 Oglala Lakota tribespeople and followers of the American Indian Movement (AIM) seized and occupied the town of Wounded Knee, South Dakota, on the Pine Ridge Indian Reservation. The occupiers alleged that the administrators of the reservation were corrupt and needed to be replaced. The occupiers controlled the town for 71 days, during which time two Sioux men were shot to death by federal agents and one federal agent was paralyzed after being shot. Finally, on May 8th, about a month after the March 27th Oscars, White House officials promised to investigate their complaints, at which time the AIM leaders and their supporters surrendered.

Forty-three years later, in 2016, African American actors, in reaction to a second straight year of an all-white slate of Academy Award nominees, embarked on a protest hash tagged OscarsSoWhite, calling out the lack of representation of people of color in Hollywood.

At that time, the popular actress Jada Pinkett Smith was quoted as saying she'd found affirmation for her own decision to boycott the Oscars by watching a clip of Sacheen Littlefeather's 1973 appearance at the Oscars on Marlon's behalf.

Today, of course, the era of "Shut up and Shoot the Ball" is long over. Celebrities are at the forefront of all social and cultural movements; they are expected to be there. In many ways, Marlon's history has been America's history. In every way he has been a forerunner.

At Marlon's funeral, Native American activist Russell Means spoke emotionally about the meaning of Marlon's early support. "It's not possible for you to understand how inferior we felt, how we were made to feel. We were the enemies of the American government. We were drunks. We were ne'er-do-wells. We were nothing."

When Marlon made the grand gesture of refusing his Oscar, Means said, "For the first time, those beleaguered men and women (participating in the siege) at Wounded Knee thought that maybe, finally, some white man got it, some white man was willing to say that this was his issue, too, that it was an American issue." The Native Americans who watched the Oscar telecast, Means said, felt unexpected joy. "We never dreamt that he would turn (the moment) over to us. We started to scream and cry."

According to the film critic Pauline Kael, beginning in the 1950s, "Brando represented the ultimate rebel, a reaction against the post-war mania for security. As a protagonist, the Brando of the early fifties had no code, only his instincts. He was a development from the gangster leader and the outlaw. He was antisocial because he knew society was crap; he was a hero to youth because he was strong enough not to take the crap. Brando represented a contemporary version of the free American."

He is gone, but ever with us.

***

A few years ago, I was having a drink with a trio of younger writers. We were at a bar near their alma mater, the Missouri School of Journalism, where we were giving a seminar; for good reason they had received a hero's welcome.

Among them was Wright Thompson, a talented and well-decorated ESPN writer and author who worked closely with Jay Lovinger for many years. I'd never actually met him before this trip, but it didn't matter. We fell into step like long-lost cousins, blood-relations through Jay.

The place was loud. I remember the walls were brick. I think I was at the head of the table, two guys on my left side, Thompson on my right.

As the evening went on, the Marlon Brando story came up. Over the course of his own career, Thompson had been sent by Lovinger on a *number* of wild goose chases. Most of them had made great stories.

"Jay talked about the Marlon Brando story all the fucking time," said Thompson—a big fuzzy bear of a man with a soft center and a lilting Mississippi drawl.

"To Jay, Marlon Brando was the perfect magazine story because it *wasn't* about Marlon Brando at all, but about celebrity and insecurity and Hollywood and all that sort of stuff. The worst thing that could have happened was you *getting* to Marlon Brando. Jay would have been terribly disappointed if you found him."

Wait a minute. What did you just say?

Not find Marlon?

I'd never, for one moment, even considered it.

As far as I knew, my assignment was to locate and interview Marlon Brando: *Go to Tahiti and find Marlon Brando.* Literally.

Never, in all the years since the first day Lovinger assigned the story, had I even imagined I wasn't expected to actually *find and interview* him.

After all, I'd learned my trade serving under guys like Woodward and Bradlee. When they gave you a job, you got it done. You never said, "I can't do that." It was *unthinkable.*

Even under my post-Marlon, amended journalistic rules of decent human being-ness, failure is not, has never been, will never be an option. You get your story no matter what. You can't come back with nothing.

But that's exactly what I did.

He went all that way, spent all that money, wrote all those words . . . and he never even interviewed Marlon Brando!

The truth is the truth. A verifiable fact. It's something I've lived with all these years.

Sure, I could hedge it a bit. I could point out that the assignment, literally, was to *find* Marlon Brando. And that's exactly what I did.

But in my own estimation, what I did was pull it out of my butt, so to speak. I typed my way out of my problem. I wrote a story about myself. In the magazine business, we call that a write-around.

Sensing the chaos raging inside my dome as my entire personal history was being updated with critical new information, Thompson spoke to me with the calming authority of a minister. "If he thought you really had a shot at getting Brando, he *never* would have green-lit the story," Thompson said.

"He never told *me* that," I croaked.

"That is so funny. That is *hilarious!*" Thompson roared. "I can't believe he didn't tell you. That's perfect! That's *classic* Jay."

I don't remember if the other guys at the table were listening in at this point or not. My sense of perspective had become distorted, as if I was looking at Thompson through a long tunnel. He seemed very small, and his voice seemed very loud.

"All these years I felt like a failure," I confessed.

"The way Jay tells it, the whole time you were gone, he was *terrified* you were going to actually get to Brando at the end." Thompson took a swig of his bourbon. Maybe it was Pappy's.

"Jay was really proud of that story. He talked about it all the time. Sure, from strictly a journalism standpoint it would have been better to find him. But from an anthropology standpoint, from a magazine standpoint, it was better not to. The worst thing that could have happened to the arc of that story was finding Marlon Brando."

***

From the start it sounded ridiculous: *Go to Tahiti and find Marlon Brando.*

I was 30 years old, divorce pending. No longer the youngest in the room, I was ready to turn the page for the big buildup. You have to dare to be bad in this world of ours, you have to try stuff, you might have to fail. One thing is certain: If you do what you've always done, it's guaranteed to turn out the same.

After nearly a decade as a journalist, I'd done a lot of stories, but what had it amounted to? Just so many clips. This time, I was hoping to write something *more* than just a story. Something big and important and lasting. Something epic. Something meaningful. Something that would seal my reputation. Change the conversation. Do a little good in the world.

As it was, Jay Lovinger suggested an all-expenses paid search for Marlon Brando, the most elusive actor of the times.

I ended up finding myself.

***

From the conclusion of *Songs My Mother Taught Me*, by Marlon Brando:

I can draw no conclusions about my life because it is a continually evolving and unfolding process. I don't know what is next. I am more surprised at how I turned out than I am about anything else. I don't ever remember trying to be successful. It just happened. I was only trying to survive. Much like a newly fertilized egg, I look now at some of the things I have done in life with astonishment. Fifty years ago, at a party at my home, I climbed out the window of my apartment in New York and clung to a balustrade eleven stories above Seventy-Second Street as a joke. I can't imagine myself ever having done that. I have difficulty reconciling the boy I was then with the man I am now. I suppose the story of my life is a search for love, but more than that, I have been looking for a way to repair myself from the damages I suffered early on and to define my obligations, if I had any, to myself and my species. Who am I? What should I do with my life? Though I haven't found answers, it's been a painful odyssey, dappled with moments of joy and laughter. In one of my letters from Shattuck, I told my parents, "In a play written by Sophocles . . . the Antigone, there are lines that say: 'Let be the future: mind the present need and leave the rest to whom the rest concerns . . . present tasks claim our care: the ordering of the future rests where it should rest.' These words written two thousand years ago are just as applicable today as they were then. It seems incomprehensible that through the fifteen thousand years since our species came into being, we have not evolved." At fifteen, I was already aware that we have learned little from our experiences, and that our proclivity is to leave the correction of wrongs and injustice to a future we are not accountable for. Yet I spent most of the next fifty-five years trying to do the opposite. Frustrated in my attempts to take care of my mother, I suppose that instead I tried to help Indians, blacks and Jews. I thought love, good intentions and positive action could alter injustice, prejudice, aggression and genocide. I was convinced that if I presented the facts—for example, show people a film that I made about starvation in India—they would be aroused and help me to alleviate that suffering. I felt a responsibility to create a better world, propelled by the certainty that compassion and love could solve its problems. I am no longer persuaded that any significant change through a course of behavior will make any difference of lasting importance. Late in life I learned something that sustains me: my suffering for other people doesn't help them. I still do what I can to be helpful, but I don't have to suffer for it. Previously I had empathized with people who were less fortunate. My sense of empathy remains undiminished, but I apply it in a different manner. Through meditation and self-examination, I feel that I am coming closer to discovering what it means to be human, and that the things I feel are the same that everybody else feels. We are all capable of hatred and of love. Curiosity about why people believe as they do is one of the most consistent features of my life. Still, I don't think any of us ever knows with certainty why we do some things or how our behavior is a product of our genes or our environment or a blend of each; it is impossible to answer the question with precision. I have not achieved the wisdom of why I am alive, and I take large comfort in the knowledge that I never will. The mist of misperception defeats all of us.

You gain a great deal simply by living long enough. In some ways I haven't changed. I was always sensitive, always curious about myself and others, always had a good instinct for people, always loved a good book and any kind of joke, which I think I learned from my parents, because they were both good laughers. But in other ways I am a vastly different person from what I was like as a child. For most of my life I had to appear strong when I wasn't, and what I wanted most was control. If I was wronged or felt diminished, I wanted vengeance. I don't anymore. I am still contemptuous of authority and of the kind of conformity that induces mediocrity, but I no longer feel a need to lash out at it. In my twenties I always wanted to be the best, but now I truly don't care. I've quit comparing myself with other people. I don't worry if somebody is more talented than I am or if people invent vicious stories about me; I understand that they're people not unlike myself who are just trying to pay the rent and who close their eyes to the vulgarity of their deeds. I realize they are doing it for their own reasons. Moreover, in telling the story of my life in this book, I must acknowledge that I am guilty of some of the sins for which I used to despise others. I believe it is fortunate that my parents died when they did; otherwise, I would have probably wrecked what was left of their lives before I found a better way to live. Now I am happier than I've ever been. My sisters and I rode out the storm together with the help of one another. Both grew into wise, independent women who beat alcoholism and created new lives for themselves. . .

"It's a long climb up Fool's Hill," my grandmother used to say about life, but Tiddy, Frannie and I made it to the top. This book, an outpouring of what was long contained, has been my declaration of liberty. I finally feel free and don't give a damn anymore what people think about me. At seventy, I'm also having more fun than ever before. The smallest details bring me joy—building or inventing something, being with my children or playing with my dog, Tim, laughing with my friends or watching an ant crawl on his way in my bathroom.

In the past few years I have rediscovered a part of me that was clean, pure and straight and had been hidden since I was a child. Somehow, I had come full circle, and I felt free. I also finally realized that I had to forgive my father, or I would be entrapped by my hatred and anguish for the rest of my life. If I didn't forgive him for the things he had done to all of us, I would never be able to forgive myself for the things I have done and felt guilty about and responsible for. Now I have forgiven him and myself, though I realize that to forgive with your mind is not always to forgive in your heart. There isn't any end to this story.

MARLON'S CHILDREN

A rigorous accounting of Marlon's children, including those he adopted, conducted by an experienced professional researcher, yields the number 11.

Two more possible children are commonly mentioned in the press and on the Internet, and included as siblings on MyHeritage. com, an online heritage research and DNA testing website. Neither have been confirmed as true Brando progeny. But just for the record:

Dylan Brando lived from 1968 to 1988. Details of his life and death are not publicly known.

Stephen Blackehart is an American actor and producer, born in Hell's Kitchen, New York, and trained at the London Academy of Music and Dramatic Art. According to some reports, he was born Stephano Brando. "I am no relation to him that I know of," Blackehart has been quoted as saying. Looking closer, Blackehart's seems to be a case where a piece of anonymous Internet graffiti finds its way into print and is later reported as fact on Wikipedia or other places around the web. An actual example of the power of *fake news*. "I've given up trying to have it taken down, but it's nonetheless untrue," Blackehart said.

Marlon's first known biological child, Christian Devi Brando, was born in 1958. He was named after Marlon's longtime friend (and lover, some say) the actor Christian Marquand. Christian's mother was the actress Anna Kashfi, Marlon's first wife and the author of *Brando for Breakfast*.

Kashfi was born Joan O'Callaghan in Chakradharpur, India, to a Welsh woman and her Irish husband, who worked on the Indian State railways. When she was 13, her family moved back to the UK. Later, young Joan, a beauty with dark hair and dark, almond-shaped eyes, moved to London to seek her fortune as a model. To distinguish her from the pack, an agent suggested changing her name and packaging her as an exotic ethnic.

Kashfi made her screen debut playing a Hindu woman in *The Mountain* (1956), with Spencer Tracy and Robert Wagner. In *Battle Hymn* (1957), she co-starred with Rock Hudson as a Korean girl. In *Cowboy* (1958), with Glenn Ford and Jack Lemmon, she played a Mexican. Her last film was *Night of the Quarter Moon* (1959), in which Kashfi played the African-American wife of singer Nat King Cole. Drug and alcohol problems reportedly contributed to the premature end of her acting career. The couple divorced in 1959.

In 1960, Marlon married the actress Movita Castaneda. Eight years his senior, she was an American of Mexican descent. She was said to have been born on a train traveling between Mexico and Arizona. Movita's first movie was *Flying Down to Rio* (1933), memorable for being the first film to feature the famous song and dance duo, Ginger Rogers and Fred Astaire. In a scene early in the movie, Movita sings the Carioca as the pair dances their very first cinematic number together.

Later (and synchronously), Movita played the Tahitian love interest in the pre-Marlon version of *Mutiny on the Bounty* (1935), alongside Clark Gable and Franchot Tone.

Their son, Miko Castaneda Brando, was born in 1961. Soon after, Marlon left Movita. It would eventually be discovered she was still married to her previous husband, making her union with Marlon unlawful.

Miko would grow up to a minor acting career—*Dickie Roberts: Former Child Star* (2003), and *Inchon* (1981). In *This Is It* (2009), he was listed as additional crew, due to his association with pop superstar Michael Jackson. It was as Jackson's bodyguard and personal assistant that Miko seemed to find his nitch. Because of Miko's association, Marlon in his waning years became fast friends with Jackson and spent a lot of time at the singer's fanciful Neverland Ranch—which could be seen perhaps as another celebrity's version of a private atoll.

"Dad loved Neverland," Miko was quoted as saying. "He had a 24-hour chef, 24-hour security, 24-hour help, 24-hour kitchen, 24-hour maid service. Just carte blanche."

Marlon also participated in Jackson's 30th anniversary celebration concerts in 2001, during which he gave a rambling speech which never appeared in the final cut. He also starred in Jackson's celebratory, 13-minute music video, "You Rock My World," the same year.

Marlon's third wife, who I met on Marlon's atoll, was Tarita Teriipaia. She played Movita's part in the 1962 version of *Mutiny*. When they married, she was 20 years old, 18 years younger than Brando. In order to communicate, Brando became fluent in French, her first language.

Their son, Simon Teihotu Brando, who I met in Marlon's compound on Mulholland Drive—and whose best friend, Teri'i, may or may not have seduced my Tahitian translator, causing her to flee my employ—was born in 1963. His sister, Tarita Cheyenne Brando, who I first glimpsed riding a large tractor at full speed out of a clearing in the jungle on Marlon's atoll, was born seven years later, in 1970.

In 1964, Lisa Brando was born. That she was the product of a brief union between Marlon and one Cynthia Lynn, born Zinta Valda Ziemelis in Riga, Latvia, does not seem at this point at all remarkable. In 1944, just ahead of the Soviet re-occupation of Latvia, Ziemelis fled the country with her mother. The two ended up in the U.S. in 1950. As Cynthia Lynn, Ziemelis went on to a career in Hollywood. She is best remembered for creating the role of Fräulein Helga, Colonel Klink's original secretary in *Hogan's Heroes*. She also went on to do guest appearances in such 1960s and 1970s television standards as *Gidget Grows Up*, *Mission: Impossible*, *The Odd Couple*, *Love, American Style*, and *The Six Million Dollar Man*.

In 1966, Marlon's second child with Movita was born, Rebecca Brando.

Though Marlon and Tarita divorced in 1972, she continued to reign over Teti'aroa. In 1982, Marlon adopted her daughter by another man, Maimiti Brando (born 1977), who I also met on the shores of the lagoon and at dinner, along with Tarita's niece, Raiatua Brando (born 1982), who he also adopted.

Marlon's other children include three with his long-time housekeeper, Maria Cristina Ruiz: Ninna Priscilla Brando (born May 13, 1989), Myles Jonathan Brando (born January 16, 1992), and Timothy Gahan Brando (born January 6, 1994). He also adopted Petra

Brando-Corval (born 1972), the daughter of his assistant Caroline Barrett and novelist James Clavell.

By far the greatest tragedy of Marlon's life came on the night of May 16, 1990, when his eldest son Christian Brando fatally shot the boyfriend of half-sister Cheyenne, a Tahitian named Dag Drollet. The incident occurred at Marlon's compound on Mulholland Drive. Christian was charged two days later with murder. The trial was heavily publicized. Christian's and Cheyenne's records of lifelong social and psychological difficulties were exposed. Marlon attended the Los Angeles trial every day, dogged at every step by a hoard of international press.

Before the trial, prosecutors attempted to subpoena Cheyenne to testify, arguing that her account of the shooting was crucial to prove the shooting was premeditated. Cheyenne refused to testify and fled to Tahiti. In June 1990, she gave birth to a son named Tuki Brando, presumably Drollet's child. Soon after Tuki's birth, Cheyenne twice attempted suicide and was hospitalized for drug detoxification in a psychiatric hospital. By December of that year, Cheyenne was declared "mentally disabled" by a French judge and deemed unable to testify in her brother's trial.

Without Cheyenne's testimony, prosecutors felt they could no longer prove Drollet's death was premeditated. They presented Christian Brando with a plea deal. Christian took the deal and pleaded guilty to the lesser charge of voluntary manslaughter.

Marlon took the stand on the third day of Christian's sentencing hearing. "I led a wasted life," he told the court, and went on to blame himself for the failings of his son. "Perhaps I failed as a father. There were things I could have done differently."

In February, 1991, Christian was sentenced to ten years in prison.

According to reports, Cheyenne was eventually diagnosed with schizophrenia, became isolated from her friends, and lost custody of Tuki to Tarita, who raised him in Tahiti.

In April, 1995, Cheyenne hanged herself at Tarita's house in Puna'auia, Tahiti. She is buried in a crypt belonging to the family of Dag Drollet.

Like his mother before him, Tuki went into modeling, and can be easily found on the Internet. His resemblance to Marlon (and to his mom) is striking—another young Marlon with a tan.

Christian served a total of five years and was placed on three years' probation. He was released in 1996.

Christian died of pneumonia in 2008, at 49. Though he had long struggled with drug addiction, a postmortem examination found no traces of drugs in his system.

"Hunting Marlon Brando" was first published in a shorter form in the *Washington Post Magazine*, July 5, 1987, and then again in 2008 in *Wounded Warriors*, published by Da Capo Press. Published with the permission of the author.

Also by Mike Sager

NONFICTION

Scary Monsters and Super Freaks: Stories of Sex, Drugs, Rock 'n' Roll, and Murder

Revenge of the Donut Boys: True Stories of Lust, Fame, Survival, and Multiple Personality

The Someone You're Not: True Stories of Sports, Celebrity, Politics & Pornography

Stoned Again: The High Times and Strange Life of a Drugs Correspondent

Vetville: True Stories of the U.S. Marines at War and at Home

The Devil and John Holmes - 25th Anniversary Author's Edition: And Other True Stories of Drugs, Porn and Murder

Janet's World: The Inside Story of Washington Post Pulitzer Fabulist Janet Cooke

Travels with Bassem: A Palestinian and a Jew Find Friendship in a War-Torn Land

The Lonely Hedonist: True Stories of Sex, Drugs, Dinosaurs and Peter Dinklage

Tattoos & Tequila: To Hell and Back with One of Rock's Most Notorious Frontmen

Shaman: The Mysterious Life and Impeccable Death of Carlos Castaneda

FICTION

Deviant Behavior, A Novel

High Tolerance, A Novel

About the Author

Mike Sager is a best-selling author and award-winning reporter. A former *Washington Post* staff writer and contributing editor to *Rolling Stone*, he has written for *Esquire* for more than thirty years. Sager is the author or editor of more than a dozen books, including anthologies, novels, a biography, and textbooks. In 2010 he won the National Magazine Award for profile writing. Several of his stories have inspired films and documentaries; he is editor and publisher of The Sager Group LLC. For more information, please see MikeSager. com

About the Publishers

NeoText is a publisher of quality fiction and long-form journalism. Visit the NeoText website at NeoTextCorp.com.

The Sager Group was founded in 1984. In 2012 it was chartered as a multimedia content brand, with the intent of empowering those who create art—an umbrella beneath which makers can pursue, and profit from, their craft directly, without gatekeepers. TSG publishes books; ministers to artists and provides modest grants; and produces documentary, feature, and commercial films. By harnessing the means of production, The Sager Group helps artists help themselves. For more information, please see TheSagerGroup.net.

THE SAGER GROUP

Artifex Te Adiuva

Made in the USA
Middletown, DE
21 February 2021